M000168008

Kaua'i

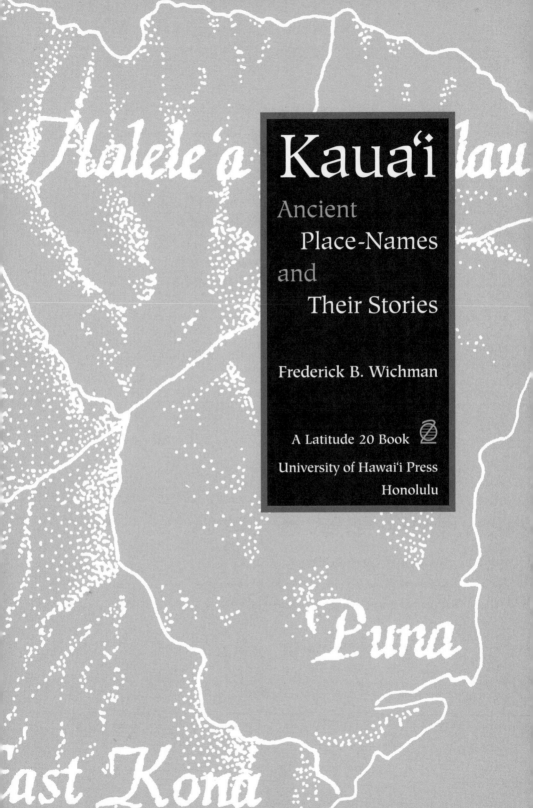

Kaua'i

Ancient
Place-Names
and
Their Stories

Frederick B. Wichman

A Latitude 20 Book

University of Hawai'i Press
Honolulu

Library of Congress Cataloging-in-Publication Data

Wichman, Frederick B., 1928–

   Kaua'i : ancient place-names and their stories /
Frederick B. Wichman.

      p.   cm.

   "A latitude 20 book."

   Includes bibliographical references and index.

   ISBN 0–8248–1943–8 (pbk. : alk. paper)

   1.   Folklore—Hawaii—Kauai.   2.   Names,
Geographical—Hawaii—Kauai.   3.   Kauai (Hawaii)—
Name.   I.   Title.

GR110.H38W47   1998

919.6941'001'4—dc21   97–45775

                                             CIP

University of Hawai'i Press books are printed on
acid-free paper and meet the guidelines for permanence
and durability of the Council on Library Resources

Designed by Jim Wageman, Wigwag

Photographs by David Boynton

Maps by Christine Fayé

To my children and grandchildren

Contents

CONTENTS

Preface

*W*hen the first Polynesians stepped ashore on Kaua'i, they began to name the land they had come to settle. Over a period of almost two thousand years, each ridge, each valley, each *ahupua'a* became filled with the names and stories of people who have walked this island. In the past two hundred years, names in a new language have begun to replace the old. Sugar plantations identified their fields for their own use. Surfers have renamed the areas of great waves, and often the adjacent land also took on these names. Where, to the *kama'āina,* are Majors, Donkey Beach, and Tunnels? A new culture has imposed itself on the old and is pushing it aside. The ancient place-names, however, tell of a rich and wondrous heritage, and they are in great danger, like many of the island's plants and birds, of disappearing forever.

This collection of place-names and of the stories connected to them comes from storytellers past and present, from dusty files in libraries and archives, and from out-of-print books. I built a list of place-names by searching maps, beginning with the U.S. Government Survey maps, followed by the maps of Kaua'i in the State of Hawai'i Accounting Department. The Archives of Hawai'i yielded the Māhele records from the first claim letters to the testimonies of witnesses, filled with place-names. Both the Andrews and Pukui-Elbert dictionaries yielded names and stories. So did Fornander's *Collection of Antiquities and Hawaiian Folklore*, as well as Emerson's *Unwritten Literature* and its invaluable notes. Ruth Hori of the Bishop Museum Library opened her files containing Francis Gay's *Place-names of Kaua'i*, the stories of the Mū people in Wainiha, Kapo-'ula-kina'u's journey around Kaua'i, and the research in 1885 of Lahainaluna students on Kaua'i. Sigrid Southworth of the Kamehameha Schools Library found the original papers submitted for a prize offered by Martha Beckwith, noted anthropologist and author of *Hawaiian Mythology.* My search grew in scope and reached into privately held manuscripts, Hawaiian newspaper articles, and conversations with *kupuna* willing to share their knowledge. The search is not finished; there are still many people to question and many old papers to read.

There are countless more place-names on Kaua'i than are contained in this volume. Every agricultural field had a name, peaks and hills were named, boulders were named, and it is obvious that many names are forever lost. The life of this land is preserved in its place-names. Let them be remembered.

My children pointed out that I had been remiss myself not to tell them stories of their Hawaiian heritage I had heard as a child growing up in Wailua-uka from such storytellers as my grandfather Charles A. Rice and from Charlie Huddy at Pihanakalani Ranch. When I was an adolescent at Hā'ena, Jacob Maka told me wonderful stories, taking me to the actual spot where the adventures had occurred. I am deeply grateful to them. I am indebted to Esther T. Mookini, who has long encouraged me to continue to gather and share. Iris Wiley, then editor of the University of Hawai'i Press, encouraged me to write this book. Patricia Crosby, when she became my editor at the UH Press, urged me to complete the manuscript. I am also indebted to Keao NeSmith for his knowledge of the Hawaiian language and for his belief that the book should be published.

Above all, I am indebted to David Boynton, who enthusiastically roamed this island to take the photographs of many more place-name sites than appear here; Christine Fayé, who drew the interpretive maps which enrich this book; and Lorita Wichman, who has been a discerning editor of my writing. Mahalo ā nui.

Explanation

*I*n this volume, the name of a person or place is divided by hyphens at its first appearance to indicate a possible translation of the name by breaking it into separate words carrying meaning. Sometimes these divisions may not be correct. Only if the story of the naming is known can the translation be considered accurate. Otherwise the translation remains an educated guess presented as an aid to non-Hawaiian-speaking readers. After the first appearance, the name is presented without the hyphens, as all names in Hawaiian are treated as one word.

Introduction

Napali   Halele'a   Ko'olau

West Kona

Puna

East Kona

The Polynesians of **Kaua'i Kuapapa**, "ancient Kaua'i," were descendants of an ancient people who had migrated from island to island across the Pacific Ocean seeking new homelands. They traveled in double-hulled canoes, some of which were capable of carrying 120 people and all the supplies needed for the voyage, as well as the familiar food plants and animals needed in their new homes.

The ancestors of the people of Kaua'i had settled for a time in the Fiji islands. Then the Chiefess Papa married Wākea, a chief of a distant land. Wākea brought new ideas and customs, beginning a struggle between the older line and a new order. Wākea's beliefs included the separation of chiefs from commoners and the creation of a slave class separate from both. Religious *kapu* (taboos) restricting the activities of women were imposed. A priesthood developed whose purpose was to help control the behavior of the people and subordinate them to their chiefs.

The resulting conflict between new and old once again sent settlers into the Pacific Ocean searching for a new homeland. These voyagers were observers of nature, using the stars, waves, currents, and cloud formations to guide them. Bird flight, green reflection on cloud bottoms indicating land, and the red glow of volcanoes lured them into the unknown Pacific Ocean to find the countless islands of Polynesia.[1]

Papa's name was given to the *papakū,* the foundations under the seas from which new lands arose. She in time became the central person in the successive generations of the *ali'i* (the chiefly class) that reached from the ancient world of the gods to the present. This was an unbroken genealogical line that gave the *ali'i* their *mana* (spiritual and political power) and their authority over the *maka'āinana* (the people who actually worked the land).

During the twelve generations after Papa and Wākea, the island of Nuku Hiwa in the Marquesas group was settled by voyagers either from Sāmoa or directly from Fiji. In turn, Nuku Hiwa sent out voyagers who found the Society Islands to the south. Ki'i, a chief of Tahiti, sent his sons, 'Ulu and Nana'ulu, on voyages of discovery. 'Ulu and his descendants found and populated many islands of the South Pacific. Nana'ulu followed the winds northward and discovered the islands of Hawai'i, and his descendants flourished in these lands, rich with water and arable land.

Kaua'i *ali'i* traced their ancestry from Nana'ulu. The *mana*, both the spiritual and political power descending through this line, was stronger than any other because it was the most ancient genealogy known. As a result, Kaua'i has always been the most fiercely independent of the Hawaiian islands. It was a land of fearless raiders who dared sail out of sight of land while others crept from island to island. Kaua'i nurtured the most beautiful chiefesses, the bravest heroes, the strongest warriors, and the fiercest giants. It was an island where gods and demigods were a part of daily life and where they lived, fought, and loved could easily be pointed out to unbelievers.

When this archipelago was found, the largest island, Hawai'i, was named in honor of Hawai'i-loa, a legendary and heroic discoverer of new lands. One of the volcanoes on this large island was named Hualālai after his wife, and the islands of Maui, Moloka'i, and O'ahu were named after his older children. Kaua'i was the youngest and favorite child of Hawai'iloa. As such, he was perhaps carried on his father's shoulders, hence offering a possible translation of **Kau-'a'i** as "place around the neck."[2] Kaua'i's wife was Wai-'ale-'ale, and her name was given to the large central massif and its small lake near the crest of the island's tallest peak, where she was buried.

The new settlers brought their histories and place-names with them. As they named the geographical features of this new home, they used ancient names to suggest that present and future actions should reflect the standards of the past. Each island thus became the historical repository of all the former homelands.

As the generations rolled by, each mountain, ridge, valley, and stream was named, as well as unusual rocks, groves of trees—indeed, every corner of the land on which the people lived. These names were used to tie the people to their environment and to places where *mauli ola* (the sacred essence of life) was to be found. Tools, occupations, physical features, and the description of cultural usage left their names on house sites, pasturelands, and farming fields. Certain names recall the men and women whose actions proved worthy of remembrance.

These names for us today are windows into the past, recalling the history, environment, and culture of the long succession of people who inhabited the land of Kaua'i Kuapapa.

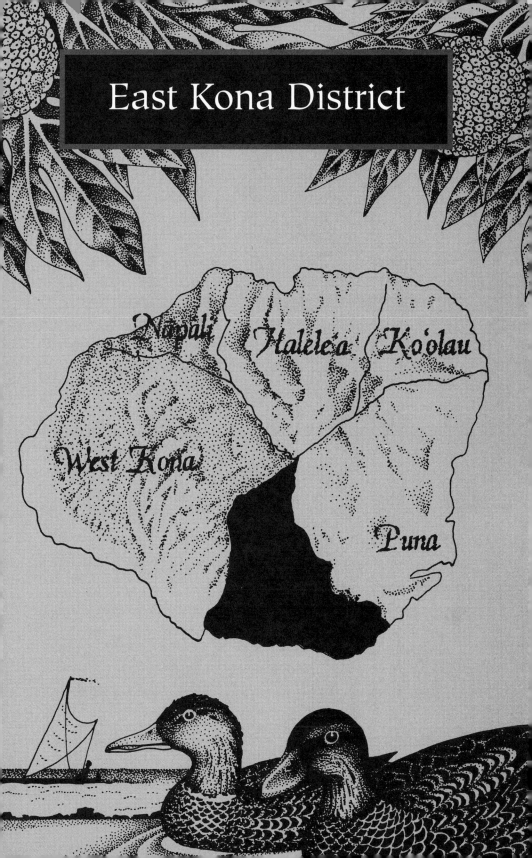

East Kona District

Napali Halele'a Ko'olau

West Kona

Puna

*O*ver the years, as the population increased and the need for governmental control developed, Kaua'i was divided into five large districts. Each of these districts was further divided into many *ahupua'a* (land units that began at a point in the mountains and followed a watershed down ridges to the sea). Each included all the natural resources needed by its inhabitants, from fishing grounds in the sea to forests in the mountains. Each was independently self-sustaining, exporting only the goods for the support of the chiefs and priests.

The largest of these districts is Kona, containing twelve *ahupua'a*. Kona occupies the entire south shore of the island, stretching from the cliffs of Nāpali on the west to the Hā'upu Range in the east. The land gently stretches upward from the sandy beaches through what was once an open grassy plain with scattered trees to the soaring ridges leading to the highest peak of the island, **Ka-wai-kini**, "multitudinous water," 5,243 feet above sea level. The rainfall is heavy here, averaging 450 inches a year, feeding a large swamp, the **Alaka'i**, "to lead."

The most distinctive feature of Kona is a huge canyon complex dug out by the constant flow of rainwater. Several deep canyons open into one large one, the Waimea. Each of these high-walled valleys provided a safe and pleasant living space to an ever-increasing population. Waimea Canyon shrinks to a narrow opening between two ridges, a feature that created a population unique in Hawai'i, one that had no access to the sea and had to barter their tools and woodenware for seafood.

Waimea

The first known settler of Kaua'i, Kū'alu-nui-kini-ākea, chose Waimea Valley for his new home.[1] The shallow sea between Kaua'i and Ni'ihau teemed with fish, the river delivered fresh water and food, and the even climate was warm, ideal for growing crops, and comfortable to a people who wore a minimum of clothing.

The river and the canyon were called **Wai-mea**, "red water," because of the color of the dirt carried by the river in flood. A mile up from its mouth, the Waimea is joined by another river: **Wai-kea,** "white water." For a while the two streams do not mingle. The water on the left is the color of iced tea, while on the right the water is clear. The red side was called **Ka-wai-'ula-'ili-ahi,** "water that turns the skin red as fire."[2]

These first settlers worshiped Kāne, god of sun and freshwater, and thus of all living things. The few *kānāwai* (laws) concerned the preservation of agricultural and marine resources. All ceremonies in the *heiau* (temple) were simple and the audience participated in all the rites. *Heiau* were built so that all priestly ceremonies could be seen by the assembled people who participated in the rites. From the beginning, there was a lack of distinction among the Kaua'i *ali'i* (chiefs). The rank of the mother determined in large part the rank of her child.

The government was led by the *ali'i nui* (ruling chief), who acted as a wise patriarch or respected village elder. It was possible for commoners unhappy with their *ali'i nui* to dispose of him and take on a new chief. They could also move to another district where another *ali'i* ruled. The *ali'i nui* was aided by a counselor, *ali'i'ai moku* (an adviser on political affairs), and a head priest, *kahuna nui,* who controlled the religious rites and ceremonies that were an integral part of daily life.

The first settlers brought their food plants with them—about thirty in all. Where these plants were first grown remains in the names of fields beside the river: **Kumu-kukui,** "source of candlenut," a tree that provided oil for lamps, nuts for food and medicine, dyes, and lumber; **Kumu-niu,** "source of coconuts," which yielded drink, food, fronds for thatching and weaving, coir for cordage, lumber, and drinking cups; **Kumu-'ulu,** "source of breadfruit," which gave a dye, a breadlike food, and lumber; **Kumu-hau,** "source of hau," used for medicine, net floats, and cordage—a tree of a thousand and one uses; **Kumu-'ōhi'a,** "source of *'ōhi'a,*" the mountain apple tree that provides abundant red and white fruit that can be dried in the sun and will last for months.

Kū'alu-nui-paukū-mokumoku followed his father Kū'alunuiki-niākea as *ali'i nui*. He sent back to his homeland for a people called Menehune, who were masters of stonework and engineering. The Menehune were an energetic, short but broad-shouldered, muscular people. They were organized in divisions based upon their skills and work duties and were completely obedient to their leaders. They worked as a team and if a project was interrupted for any reason, they abandoned it and never returned to finish it. Under Kū'alunuipau-kūmokumoku, many *heiau*, fishponds, and irrigation systems for wet-land farming were built. These Menehune explored the island from one side to the other and left the stories of their adventures in place-names that still remain.[3]

The son of Kū'alunuipaukūmokumoku was Ola. He opened the land between the ridges and the sea to agriculture. The land was considerably higher than the river, and separating the rich bottomland from freshwater was the cliff **Pali-uli**, "green cliff," which rose directly from the riverbed. The original Paliuli was the paradise of the gods here on earth. If the gods so wished, Paliuli could float above the clouds, or it could rest upon the earth or ocean, or even sink beneath the sea. Here the gods made the first man and woman, but as these two displeased the gods, Kāne in his albatross form drove them away into the ocean and hid Paliuli from them. A giant *mo'o* (lizard), Kiha-nui-lūlū-moku, lay atop the cliff and guarded the land below.[4]

Ola gathered the Menehune and asked that an irrigation ditch be built around Paliuli. The Menehune chief, Papa-'ena'ena,[5] said they would build the ditch as long as every Menehune worker would be fed the same food at the end of the construction. Ola agreed.

The Menehune first hollowed out a huge stone and brought it to the beach where Papa'ena'ena could sit on top and direct the work. This rock has unfortunately been moved and its whereabouts are unknown. The Menehune quarried stone from Mokihana Ridge across the river. These were huge—some three feet wide and five feet long. Each was

KĪKĪAOLA

smoothed and prepared in such a way that a peg on one stone fit into a hole on another. These dressed stones were placed in the riverbed and built up until there was a platform wide enough for the irrigation ditch and a path. When it was complete, the water was let in, and it flowed around the cliff twenty feet above river level to the waiting land. This ditch was called Kīkī-a-Ola, "container acquired by Ola."[6]

The new farmland was named after their ancient homeland, Pe'e-Kaua'i, "hidden Kaua'i." It was divided into four areas: Ka-mo'o-kahi, "first land division"; Ka-mo'o-'elua, "second land division"; Ka-mo'o-'ekolu, "third land division"; and Ka-mo'o-'eha, "fourth land division." Imaginative place-names came only after the original settlers were assured of a steady food production.

The landing on the west side of the river mouth was named Ke-ahi-lele, "flying fire," perhaps after a shooting star or a comet that marked their arrival. On the opposite side was Lā'au-'ōkala, "thorny tree."

Poli-o-lehua, a mermaid, used to sit on a rock at Lā'au'ōkala combing her hair. She was beautiful and many young men over the centuries tried to woo her, but she always refused them. When they grew too importunate, she would dive into the water where no one could find her. After many centuries, however, a young chief dove after her and followed her into her cave. She was so afraid that she left, never to return.[7]

Upriver of Lā'au'ōkala is a small plain edged on one side by twenty-foot-high cliffs. This is **Māha'iha'i**, "brittle." On this plain Ka-iki-pa'a-nanea, a descendant of Ola, had a large sports field. He excelled in feats of physical strength, especially boxing and wrestling, for he was a large, strong man. He always demanded a full crowd of spectators at all sports events, which were held often, and everyone had to leave their work to attend. In addition, Kaikipa'ananea refused to be bothered with the necessary religious observances, and the land and people began to suffer because of it. If a man actually outboxed him, he would challenge him to a game of riddles. He had three riddles, and whoever could not give the correct answer to all three was burned alive in a fire pit.

Kaikipa'ananea was so cruel that no Kaua'i woman would marry him, so he sent some men to find—and if necessary kidnap—a woman from one of the windward islands. The woman they brought back, however, already had a husband—one of the famous heroes of Maui. This man, Ka-paka-'ili-'ula, followed his wife to Kaua'i and stayed with a chief who lived near the court. Kapaka'ili'ula befriended Kaikipa'ananea's servant, a man who was reviled and despised by all. Kapaka'ili'ula's gestures of friendship meant so much that the servant told him the answer to the three riddles. Kapaka'ili'ula challenged Kaikipa'ananea to duels of boxing and wrestling. Much to Kaikipa'ananea's dismay, he lost. He then challenged Kapaka'ili'ula to the riddling contest, but Kapaka'ili'ula knew the answers and the cruel chief ended up in his own fire pit.[8]

A small stream flowed over the cliff of Māha'iha'i into a deep pool. This cascade was called **Wai-lele**, "waterfall," and the last king of Kaua'i, Kaumuali'i, enjoyed jumping from the cliff into the pond below.

When Congregational missionaries Samuel Whitney and Samuel Ruggles arrived in 1820, King Kaumuali'i built them a home at Māha'iha'i. But from time to time this home was flooded, and they were glad to accept land on the other side of the river at 'Āhui-manu, "flock of birds," named after the thousands of wading birds that lived in the marshes to the west.[9]

After he became governor of Kaua'i under the conquering Kamehameha dynasty, Ka-iki-o-'Ewa satisfied his desire to indulge himself in Western goods by ordering every man, woman, and child into the mountains to cut down sandalwood trees. He left no one to tend the food crops. The wood was brought to 'Āhuimanu plain and piled up in the size and shape of a ship's hold. This pile of wood, and many others, left a name, **Pu'u-wahie**, "firewood hill," in remembrance.

Sandalwood had first been discovered by Captain Kendrick, a Yankee trader, in 1791. He had taken on firewood at Waimea. Just after the ship had passed Ni'ihau, the cook fired up his stove and Capt. Kendrick immediately recognized the smell of sandalwood. Unable to return to Ni'ihau because of contrary winds, Kendrick sent three sailors back with instructions to gather all the sandalwood they could find and wait for his return.[10] The three sailors—John Williams, a Welshman who had joined Capt. Kendrick's ship in China, James Coleman, an Irishman who claimed to have been born in New York, and Rowbottom, a 16-year-old from Derbyshire, England—returned to Kaua'i but were not successful in getting sandalwood.[11] Capt. Kendrick did not return for five years and the men became destitute. Kaumuali'i took them into his circle of friends and they became advisers on the ways of the white man. Williams was hated by Yankee traders for he advised Kaumuali'i of the true value of the goods being offered.[12] Williams was called Uilama and married Mere. They had no children and he died while Kaikio'ewa was governor. His houselot near Pu'uwahie was named **Holoa-wiki**, "quick decision."[13]

Looking upward from the beach, there are two intermittent streams between three ridges. The farthest west of the three is **Ke-olo-'ewa.** Keolo'ewa was a god of sorcerers and of black magic who was said to possess people. This god was represented by a block of wood on which was set a neck and head made of wickerwork. This frame was covered with red feathers, the helmet was covered with human hair, and its large, distended mouth was filled with shark's teeth.[14]

The Inner Canyons

Branching off the Waimea River to the east are four major valleys. The first is **Makaweli,** which became a separate *ahupua'a.* **Mokihana,** "*mokihana* shrub," is named after the fragrant endemic berry. Third is **Wai-'alae,** "mudhen stream." The name encompasses the stream, the waterfall, and the mountainous area at its back. The *'alae* is a black wading bird with a red forehead. It was considered an *'aumakua* (family guardian) by many families. An *'alae's* call was an omen of ill fortune or imminent death to anyone who heard it. If a priest heard an *'alae* call before he had finished with his prescribed set of prayers, the prayers had to be started over again, no matter how close to the end he was.

The fourth branch is **Koai'e,** named after the tree that was uprooted in this valley by Nā-maka-o-ka-pao'o, who made a war club out of it. Nāmakaokapao'o was a hero who for a short time was ruler of Hawai'i island.[15] The *koai'e* is a relative of the *koa* but has much harder wood that was used for tapa beaters, canoe paddles, and spears. The valley was heavily populated and its inhabitants were considered country cousins. "*He koai'e!*"— "He's a *koai'e!*"—was said to refer to somebody as a backwoodsman.[16]

Upstream was **Mau-lili,** "constant jealousy." Below a small waterfall lies a rock with two shiny spots, **Nā-maka-o-ka-ʻōpae,** "eyes of the shrimp." In ancient times there was a woman who lost her husband to a rival. The woman asked her grandmother what to do. Following her advice, the woman killed her rival while she was bathing in the stream by throwing a rock down on her head. The rival's eyes popped out and floated down the stream. When the husband, who was fishing below, stooped to see what these shining objects were, his wife threw a boulder down on him, killing him. She placed the eyes in his mouth. The rival and the husband were turned to stone and can still be seen, the husband with the shiny eyes still in his mouth.[17]

Just north of Maulili there is a waterfall with a deep cave behind it, its entrance covered by the water. This waterfall is named **Kōmaliu** after the daughter of a Waimea chief. A chief named Mano wanted Kōmaliu as his wife. She knew him to be cruel and refused him. He kidnapped her and brought her to this cave. Day after day he asked her to marry him, but she always refused. Finally he killed her. Her blood trickled into the waterfall and flowed down the river. Kōmaliu's blood colors the entire river, thus accounting for the name **Wai-mea,** "red water."[18]

The Road through Alakaʻi Swamp

Climbing the western edge of Waimea Canyon into the mountains brings a traveler to a 3,662-foot-high cinder cone whose name was originally pronounced **Puʻu-kāpele,** "distended hill." The hill is so named because of its resemblance to the characteristic distended bellies of the Menehune, many of whom lived in this area. In later years, after Pele arrived and became a goddess, the name became **Puʻu-ka-Pele,** "volcano hill." Pele is said to have stamped her foot on top of this hill when she leaped across the channel to Oʻahu, which formed the crater found at its summit. Sometimes this cone is called **Puka-Pele,** "Pele's doorway."

This was the site of a permanent settlement, for koa and koaiʻe trees were farmed here. The wood was carved into canoes and paddles.

PU'UKĀPELE

Because of the beauty of these trees, whenever a handsome youth was seen, people said in admiration, *He keiki kālai hoe no ka uka o Pu'ukāpele.* "A paddle-making youth of Pu'ukāpele."[19] However, if someone felt he was being taken for a fool, his riposte was, *'A'ole au ke kālai hoe no Pu'ukāpele.* "I am no paddle maker from Pu'ukāpele."[20]

Pu'ukāpele was the home of the Menehune. They often gathered together in this place to talk, which has given rise to another saying indicating that small murmurings can be heard at faraway points:

> *Wāwā ka Menehune i Pu'ukāpele ma Kaua'i, puoho ka manu o ka loko o Kawainui ma Ko'olaupoko, O'ahu.* "The hum of the voices of the Menehunes at Pu'ukāpele, Kaua'i, startled the birds of Kawainui pond at Ko'olaupoko, O'ahu."[21]

A man and a woman, both commoners, spent the night of Kāne at Puʻukāpele and they slept together under the trees. Kalani, another commoner, caught sight of them and ran to a small tree close to where they were lying in order to see them more clearly. He didn't realize that he, too, was watched and afterward where Kalani had stood was known as **Ka-ule-kola**, "sexually excited penis," after the state of Kalani's genitals. The story was told both as an amusing incident and as a moral that seeking a little more privacy might be a good thing.[22]

Ola, the most renowned of the early chiefs, and the Menehune first settled Puʻukāpele and there are many place-names reflecting their history here. Once some Menehune were carrying two canoes down to the beach. They attempted to cross a deep, steep-sided ditch without supporting the canoes properly. When the canoe prows were on one bank and the sterns on the other, the canoes broke in the middle and fell into the gully. There they were turned to stone and filled with dirt to make an easy crossing. The Menehune in charge of this disaster ran for his life, but he was caught and turned into the stone **Pōhā-kā-i-nā-puaʻa**, "stone against which to dash the hogs," but the story of this name is lost.[23]

A small valley at Puʻukāpele is named **Kapuahi-o-Ola**, "fireplace of Ola." Not long ago there was still the outline of a specially built fireplace said to date from Ola's time. Nearby is **Ka-hālau-o-Ola**, "canoe shed of Ola," no doubt where Ola's canoe was stored while it was being carved out.

Ahu-loulu, "heap of loulu palms," was the *heiau* of Puʻukāpele.[24] It had four-foot thick walls. There was a paved enclosure at the back where there is a large rock. The plugged-up holes in this rock indicate it may have been used as a birthstone, a place where the umbilical cords of newly born children were placed for safekeeping. The loulu, a Pritchardia, was an endemic palm.

A few miles above Puʻukāpele is **Hale-manu**, "bird house," where bird catchers lived while they hunted Kauaʻi's unique bird family, the

KANALOAHULUHULU

brilliantly colored honeycreepers that lived in the *'ōhi'a lehua* forests. Especially prized were the yellow-green *'amakihi* and *'anianiau,* the bright yellow *'akialoa* and *nukupu'u,* the orange-red *'i'iwi* or *olokele,* and the deep crimson *'apapane.* High chiefs wore ceremonial helmets, capes, and cloaks made of these brilliant feathers. Chiefesses draped feathered wreaths around their heads and necks. Each of these garments was created by tying countless feathers to a background of knotted fiber netting. Very few of these birds, endemic to this island, still flit through the forest.

A little farther on there is a meadow, **Kanaloa-huluhulu,** "hairy Kanaloa." All roads through the mountains—the road from Waimea, the road leading to the valleys of Nāpali, and the one running through the Alaka'i Swamp to Wainiha—joined at this meadow. This was an easily recognized place on the ancient road because no trees grew here, which is unusual in this land of thick forest. Several stories were told to explain this important place.

One story tells of a robber, **Kana-loa-huluhulu**, "hairy tall Kana," who hid among the trees, pouncing on travelers and robbing them. It became so dangerous that no one could travel on the road. The *ali'i nui* of Waimea sent his constable, who recognized the robber as a *kupua* (a person with supernatural powers). The two fought, but the robber was no match for a trained warrior and soon was killed with a blow of a war club. The constable cut off the giant's head and tossed it into the canyon on his way back to Waimea. At dusk, the giant returned to life, as giants in those days could do, but he could not find his head. He felt around him and whenever he found a tree, he uprooted it, feeling for his head among the roots. By dawn, the area was completely bare of trees. It is said even now that no trees grow here for Kanaloahuluhulu will always tear them out by their roots, still looking for his head.[25]

Another story says that the god Kanaloahuluhulu had to spend the night here under the *'ōhi'a lehua* trees. He laid down under a tree and fell asleep. During the night a gentle rain began, as it often does, and the raindrops gathered on the leaves and dropped onto his head. Kanaloa was angry to be awakened, tore up the tree by its roots, and moved under another tree. The raindrops continued to drip on the god's head. Each time he awoke, angrier than before, the god uprooted the tree under which he was sleeping. By morning he had torn up all the trees, and since then no trees have dared to grow here for fear of Kanaloa's anger.[26]

The main road around the island, which was really nothing more than a path, continued over a small ridge into **Wai-neki**, "giant bulrush water," a stream that feeds into the **Kōke'e**, "to wind and bend," which now gives the whole area its name. In this valley, Limaloa, a chief who lived about 1350 A.D., built some houses with Menehune help that are noted for their orderliness. Nothing else is known of this village. The road continues to the stream 'Ele-keni-nui, "great dark silent place." On the left of its source is **Kapu-ka-'ōhelo**, "sacred is the 'ōhelo berry," and on the right is **Kapu-ka-'ōhelo-lau**, "sacred are the 'ōhelo leaves." The 'ōhelo is a small shrub bearing red or yellow berries that are delicious. In these woods lived a man and his wife, together with their beloved daughter, who had a happy disposition and whose cheeks were red from playing in the dappled sun day after day. One day she grew ill and a high fever began to waste her away. Her father left to search for a doctor to cure his daughter. He met a man just below Pu'ukāpele who claimed to be a doctor and said he could cure the girl. First, however, he demanded payment: fish from the sea and shrimp from Koai'e Canyon. These the man got with great difficulty, and he then led the doctor to his daughter's bedside. But, being a charlatan, nothing the false doctor could do saved the girl. Soon after her death, Lono-pūhā happened to pass by. He was the god of healing and medicine. He knew he could have saved the girl if he had come in time, and he listened with growing anger as the man told the story of the charlatan he had found. Lonopūhā, as befitted a god, turned the false doctor into a boulder and turned the girl into the first 'ōhelo plant. It is a plant that reproduces in its sweet red berries the rosy cheeks of the beloved girl.[27]

Many years later, before she turned into a goddess, red-haired Pele came to 'Elekeninui with two guides. They quarreled violently over which way to go to find food and shelter. Pele saw birds eating some red berries and picked some for her supper. She laid down, told her guides, "Angry words do not fill stomachs!" and went to sleep. From then on, 'ōhelo berries were the sacred food and choice offering to Pele, volcano goddess, even though an enemy teased her about eating bird-food.[28]

The road plunges into a steep narrow gulch, **Ka-ua-i-ka-nanā**, "rain defied." During a storm, a bird catcher entered **Ke-'akū**, a small cave named after a native lobelia tree that grew nearby. This cave was big enough for only one person, so his companion had to stand under a tree where he became soaking wet and grew colder by the minute. This man thought and thought and finally had a great idea. He shouted into the rain, *Ua 'oe eka ua, ka ua o ka nanā keia!* "You are the rain, a rain defied is this!"[29] The man in the cave thought his companion had found better shelter than he had and he ran out to see where it was. The man under the tree rushed into the cave, and thus it was the first man who had to spend the night out in the rain.[30]

From this valley the trail winds onto **Ka-walawalania**, "burning pain," an apt name for the feeling in one's stomach upon crossing a ridge only a foot or so across, where on the left the traveler looks down several hundred feet into Kauaikananā and on the right equally far down into the valley of **Ka-wai-kōī**, "rushing stream."

Before starting through the swamp, travelers must not pick *'ōhi'a lehua* leaf buds or its flowers, for that will cause a thick white fog to conceal the road. They should also be warned not to throw stones at any of the small birds that live here, for they will cause a misty rain to fall that has very fine drops and looks like smoke, quickly soaking travelers and chilling them.

Soon one reaches the swamp **Ka-lehua-makanoe**, "misty *lehua* blossom." The *'ōhi'a lehua* trees here grow only one or two feet tall and honeycreepers and butterflies flit from tree to tree almost underfoot. Beneath these tiny trees grow the native violet, *nani Wai'ale'ale,* and an insect-eating sundew plant. The trail winds across the bog but twists and turns around the deep pools and mudholes that come and go according to the latest rainfall.

At the other end of this swamp there used to be a very tall, twisted *'ōhi'a lehua* named **Kūkala-a-ka-manu**, "announcement of the bird." The birds must have laughed at the mud-covered travelers floundering through the swamp. They knew that the worst was yet to come.

19

The trail winds down to cross Kawaikōī. Then it zigzags up the hill until it comes to a narrow clear space where there is a view across the forested swamp. This spot is named **Ka-pahu-o-Ola,** "drum of Ola." Perhaps in this confusing swampland, Ola ordered a drum to sound so that its beat would let stragglers know where the main party was resting.

Then the trail enters into the second great swamp, **'Ai-pō-iki,** "small 'Aipō, eat at night." Travelers from either direction were lucky to reach 'Aipōiki by nightfall and would hurry along as quickly as possible before the light faded to find a dry spot to spend the night, or at least a spot where the ground was solid underfoot. They would eat their meal in the darkness before passing an uncomfortable night—cold, wet, and tired.

Beyond 'Aipōiki is an even larger swamp, **'Ai-po-nui,** "large 'Aipō, eat at night." There are ponds everywhere, covered by floating hummocks of land, home of small plants and shrubs. Here and there are hills of solid land where stunted trees grow. Most of the time mists curl in and around the plants. From time to time an opening appears where the walking seems easy, but where the unwary traveler can easily become lost forever, as has happened in recent years.

Eventually one reaches **Ka-holo-ina,** "to travel making a modulated cry," where the drums were sounded with a different beat to mark the site of this large pond. In order to get around it the leader goes on ahead. When he or she is sure of the trail, the leader yells or yodels. The voice does not echo here but seems to become louder and stronger. It then becomes easy for the rest of the party to catch up.

After Kaholoina, the bogs are deep. The hammocks are small and tend to dump the traveler over as he steps on them. Chief Ola, the first explorer of this swamp, ordered tree fern trunks cut and laid down one after the other to form a corduroy road for easier walking. In a short while, the tree ferns sprouted and the road was lined with fern fronds, the **Kīpapa-a-Ola,** "Ola's pavement."

KILOHANA

Eventually one reaches the first solid bit of land, **Ka-lani-wahine,** "royal woman," named for Queen Emma. She came in the 1880s to Kaua'i and expressed a desire to cross the swamp. But there were so many people with her that night overtook them while still in the swamp. It was cold and misty. The party was discouraged and grumbled about the cold food, the cold air, the cold rain. Queen Emma began to sing, urging her people to be cheerful, and the night passed in song.[31]

Then they took to the trail again, passing **Hana-kahi,** "single task," where a false step drops the traveler into deep mud-filled ponds. They passed **Ka-'awa-ko'o,** "propped-up *'awa* plant," where the *'awa* thrown away by Ka-maile of Nu'alolo Valley was discovered centuries later by Mo'ikeha of Wailua. When they arrived at **Ka-pili-iki-a-ka-huamoa,** "short *pili* grass with the chicken egg," a narrow ditchlike place, they knew that a few steps more would bring them to **Kilohana,** "beautiful view," the lookout at the top of **Mauna-hinahina,** "gray mountain." The view is magnificent, down the length of Wainiha Valley and across to the beach of Hanalei and the crater of Kīlauea.

Makaweli

Makaweli *ahupua'a* lies to the east of Waimea and is unique in that its main river does not flow into the sea but into another river. The name **Maka-weli** has several interconnected meanings: "glaring, threatening eyes," a reference, some say, to the shining mother-of-pearl eyes of the fierce wooden idols that surrounded any *heiau* where human sacrifices were offered; "fearful eyes," of the victims themselves; and "terrifying eyes," of the idols hungry for blood.

The *ahupua'a* is large and includes several canyons descending from Alaka'i Swamp, a broad plain cut by small streams, and a shoreline that is a mixture of sand beaches and low cliffs. Today the deep valleys are home to goats and feral pigs. The remains of stone walls, irrigation ditches, and house platforms, and many of the place-names, give mute evidence of a once teeming population that inhabited these steep-sided valleys.

Such a canyon is **Moku-one**, "sand island." Mokuone Stream has its source in the Alaka'i Swamp. This valley joins the **Kahana**, "cutting," tributary, and the Makaweli Stream is born. At this junction, looking upstream, Mokuone is on the west and is a steep, narrow canyon.

About a quarter of the way up the valley is an area called **Wai-'awa'awa**, "bitter water," where the spring **Kukui-'ula**, "red candlenut tree," gives fresh water. A red kukui tree was planted here by Kahapula, the mother of Ola, after she was banished to Mokuone by her husband, Kū'alunuipaukūmokumoku. When they parted, he gave her a loincloth, a feather cape, a helmet, and a spear as gifts for their unborn son and a kukui nut that she was told to plant as soon as she arrived.[32]

Many years later, Ola was captured by the evil high priest and condemned to death. Kahapula prayed and was told to pick two kukui nuts from the tree she had planted. Then she was to juggle them in the air as she walked from Mokuone to Waiawa, a distance of at least fifteen miles. If she arrived without dropping either nut, Ola would be saved. Going slowly and carefully, with her friends and retainers clearing the path ahead of her, Kahapula succeeded.[33]

Ola is still remembered for having ordered the building of the Menehune Ditch in Waimea. In order to pay for **Kīkīaola**, the Waimea irrigation ditch, Ola promised the Menehune one shrimp each as payment for their work. Ola ordered his chief officer, Pi'i, to make sure there were enough shrimp. Naturally, Pi'i ordered every 'ōpae (shrimp) that could be found in the streams of the canyon complex to be gathered. He went himself to make sure, and in so doing, he left his name in several places.

One such place was '**Ōpae-pi'i**, "climbing shrimp" or "Pi'i's shrimp," for certainly he would have placed a taboo on all shrimp so that no one would eat them. A path in upper Mokuone is called **Ala-pi'i**, "upward path" or "Pi'i's path." Near the end of the canyon is **Hali-'ōpae**, "fetched shrimp." So it seems that the inhabitants of Mokuone where Ola had grown up provided all the shrimp they had. In the end, every Menehune did have one shrimp apiece.

The most magnificent canyon of this *ahupua'a* is **Olokele**, named after the indigenous Kaua'i honeycreeper, called *'i'iwi* nowadays. The highest cliff of this canyon rises to 3,724 feet above sea level. It is called **Ka-hōlua-manu**, "sled of Manu." Manu's parents made him do all the work preparing the family's food, from growing it to cooking it, so he had no time to learn to ride the *hōlua* (sled). This sled was about eight inches wide and its narrow platform was connected to two runners. It needed a specially constructed course down a steep hillside, usually of rocks smoothed with water-polished pebbles and covered with rushes. A *hōlua* rider would take a running start, throw himself on top of the sled, and attempt to slide down—a steep, quick, and dangerous rush straight down. Superb riders could actually stand on the sled, but a fall at that speed onto rocks often proved fatal. One day Manu watched a Menehune slide on the *hōlua*. The Menehune fell and the sled was broken. Manu repaired the sled during the little spare time he had from his parent's demands. In return, the Menehune gave him a specially crafted *hōlua* of his own. Each time Manu tried to ride his sled, his parents either threw stones onto the course or caused freshets in the stream where the course ended. Manu left them in disgust and became a famous *hōlua* rider on this slide especially built for him by the Menehune.[34]

The shoreline of Makaweli offers access to rich fishing grounds and a famous place for the sport of *he'e nalu* (surfing). The landing place for canoes was at **Ka-unu-loa**, "long endpiece of a canoe." Offshore is a rock that was once a woman named **'Ou-lehelehe**, "protruding lips." Her brother **Ka-pakohana**, "naked one," has left his name on the land area ashore of Kaunuloa on the east streambank of **Kāne-hapu'u**, "male tree fern," and his footprints in the stone at **Kapuaʻi-o-Kapakohana**, "Kapakohana's footprint." Only these names attest to a story now lost.[35]

In 1795, Kamehameha, who had just conquered the island of Oʻahu, turned his attention to an invasion of Kauaʻi. The island was ruled by a regent, ʻInamoʻo, for the fourteen-year-old Kaumualiʻi, whose parents, Ka-maka-helei and Ka-ʻeo-kū-lani, had died on an Oʻahu battlefield a few years before. Kamehameha sent an invasion fleet, but it was severely damaged by a sudden windstorm. Kamehameha then was recalled to Hawaiʻi island in the summer of 1796 to put down a revolt. Two years later ʻInamoʻo died and Kaumualiʻi's stepbrother, Keawe, captured the young chief and took over the kingdom.[36]

Among those who hastened to Keawe's side was Kiʻikikī, once the powerful second-in-command under Kaʻeokūlani. He was the *konohiki* (headman) of Wainiha and his older brother Kāne-ʻekau was *konohiki* of Hanapēpē. Kiʻikikī, during a tour around the island, shot and killed Keawe at Kapaʻa and took all the muskets, guns, and ammunition Keawe had amassed from passing whaling and merchant captains. Kiʻikikī proclaimed his allegiance to the young ruling chief Kaumualiʻi, but did not surrender the arms and ammunition. Kiʻikikī was fond of the sport of *heʻe nalu* (surfing). His favorite place was **Kaua**, "rain," off the coast of Makaweli. One day he and his brother went surfing here, leaving the calabashes of guns on the beach. The weapons were seized by Kaumualiʻi's men. Kiʻikikī saw his guns disappearing but by the time he got to shore, it was too late. He and Kāneʻekau immediately sailed to Oʻahu but were killed there by Kaumualiʻi's executioner.[37]

On the point overlooking the mouth of the Waimea river at **Hīpō**, "purge night," Russian envoy Dr. Georg Schaeffer built a fort. Dr. Schaeffer had been sent by the Russian Trading Company based in Alaska to collect either the goods or reparation for a Russian trading vessel that had gone aground at Makaweli and to look for a possible spot to establish a Russian colony. Schaeffer had dreams of himself as head of a flourishing colony. His timing was excellent. Kaumualiʻi was ill with dropsy and one of his wives was down with a fever. Schaeffer cured both quickly and earned the king's gratitude. Soon Dr. Schaeffer disclosed his intentions to establish a colony, to assist the Kauaʻi king to keep possession of his island, and to prevent American ships from trading anywhere else in the islands.

Kaumualiʻi thought Schaeffer was an official envoy of the Russians and swore allegiance to Tsar Alexander I. He returned the cargo of sealskins and paid an indemnity for them. He gave Schaeffer Hīpō and Schaeffer began to build a fort there, planted a vineyard, grew melons and tobacco, and hoped cotton would become a major agricultural export.

Schaeffer then sent some men and a ship to Oʻahu and started to build a fort and trading post in Honolulu Harbor, where the majority of the trading vessels called. Kamehameha became alarmed and sent word to Kauaʻi to rid themselves of this danger. Kaumualiʻi had no choice but to obey. Schaeffer was forcibly escorted on board his ship where he was fired upon from the guns in the fort he himself had built.[38]

Directly below the fort is **Luhi**, "tired," a beach of white sand. Here, Captain Cook's journal tells us, the first Hawaiian killed by a westerner was shot by a nervous lieutenant as Cook's crew was trying to load water and the men were jostled by an eager, curious, and—to them—threatening crowd.[39]

Farther down the coastline to the east is **Kau-makani**, "place of winds." Because of the configuration of the island, the trade winds blow directly from the east and also, following the contours of the mountains, come eddying around from the west. These winds can swirl with great force, and the ocean off Kaumakani spawns more waterspouts than anywhere else in the islands.

Hanapēpē

The Hanapēpē River is the third longest on the island and, bordered on both sides by steep canyon walls, flows directly into a bay. The river begins on the slopes of Kawaikini and cascades into **Ka-pali-emo**, "slow cliff," a gulch where the walls on both sides almost touch each other overhead. Below that is **Haulili**, "entangled," a valley where there was once a celebrated *kava* grove. The combined streams flow over **Halulu**, "rumbling," named for the noise of the waterfall echoing from the cliffs.

Within sight and sound of Halulu is **Maka-'opihi**, "eye of the *'opihi* limpet," where there is a cave in which Kawelo-'ai-kanaka lived after he was defeated by his cousin Kawelo-lei-makua. A large stone at the river crossing was **Pā-pōhaku-huna-'ahu'ula**, "stone wall in which a feather cape was hidden," a place where 'Ai-kanaka hid his symbol of rank. 'Ai-kanaka plotted his revenge as he hid here with his wife and daughter.[40]

Now the stream and valley take the name of **Kō-'ula**, "red sugarcane." Anywhere an area as small as ten square feet could be walled, it was turned into farmland. Houses were built on stone platforms to be above the floods. At the lower end of Kō'ula is a waterfall some considered the most beautiful of all: **Mana-wai-o-puna**, "stream branch of Puna." Two streams flow over the top of the cliff and join together about halfway down and drop the last hundred feet in a wide flow. The mist keeps the lichens and ferns green and moist. Today it is forgotten and unreachable, but once it was considered a necessary tourist stop.

Several miles from the sea the Kō'ula is joined by a side valley, **Manu-ahi**, "firebird." The valley was well inhabited, for every watercourse, every flat area along the stream that could be farmed—and, it seems, almost every large stone—had a name. One such stone is **Pōhā-kani**, "sounding stone." It was a large boulder with a hole

MANUAHI

through it. When it was struck with the stalk of *kī* (ti plant), it sounded like a drum and was used as a signal from one *heiau* to another. After the rebellion of 1824, Ka'ahumanu, queen regent of all the islands, sent Huleia, a former priest now converted to Christianity, to destroy every vestige of the old religion on Kaua'i. Pōhākani was on the list and Huleia broke off a part of the inside of the hole. Now, instead of shouting a resounding drumming sound, Pōhākani only whispers.[41]

Manuahi means "firebird," the *'alae*, the endemic gallinule, which had the secret of fire. The demigod Māui got the secret of fire from the bird and burned the top of the *'alae*'s head in revenge for its many lies. Since then the dark gray bird always has a fiery red streak on the top of its head.[42]

From the junction of Kō'ula and Manuahi, the Hanapēpē flows

leisurely through an ever-widening valley. This land was heavily used for farming. On the west side is **Holo-iwi**, "traveling bones," a cliff from which a high chief was once thrown by his disgruntled people to fly freely for a short period. This event—an uprising of commoners against an *ali'i*—was so rare that it takes three legends to explain it.

First, a chief of Hanapēpē lived on the top of this cliff. Each night he demanded that an infant child be delivered to him that he would use as a pillow. Naturally, the child would cry and would awaken the chief. In his anger, he would throw the infant over the cliff. Finally, his own attendants threw him over the cliff, too.[43]

A second story tells of a corpulent and crabby chief who had himself carried everywhere in a *manele* (palanquin) borne on the shoulders of four strong men. The chief would decide that he wanted to spend the night at a spot far up in the valley and his attendants would hurry to that place, build a house for the chief to sleep in, and prepare his food. On the way, the chief would change his mind and insist on sleeping and eating somewhere else and was very irritated because things were not ready. Sometimes he would insist on being carried up the Kō'ula, where his carriers struggled over the moss-covered rocks, then decide to sleep at the top of the ridge above. One evening, as the carriers struggled up the cliff carrying their burden, the chief scolded them unmercifully. Finally having had enough, the carriers threw their chief—*manele* and all—over the cliff.[44]

The more historical and probably the true event occurred when Kaweloleimakua—after he had killed his cousin 'Ai-kanaka and had been forced to kill his foster son who had betrayed him—became obsessed with finding and exterminating the children of 'Aikanaka and scoured the valleys looking for them. Alarmed at such unreasonable anger and obsession, his attendants threw him over the cliff. This event took place about 1700 A.D.[45]

Directly opposite Holoiwi on the eastern cliffs is **Ka-leina-a-ka-'uhane**, "leaping place of the soul." The souls of the dead gathered at this place and leaped over the cliff to the valley floor, where they embarked on canoes that took them to Pō, the land of the dead that lies deep in the ocean off the west end of the island.

Fittingly, on the plains of 'Ele'ele, "black," the battle that ended the separate kingdom of Kaua'i was fought. On one side were the Kaua'i chiefs still loyal to their dead king Kaumuali'i, armed with wooden war clubs, spears, daggers, and slings. Opposite them were the Kamehameha forces armed with rifles and cannon. In August 1824 the two armies fought. The Kaua'i army was destroyed, and for two weeks before amnesty was declared the Kamehameha forces sought out all the *ali'i* they could find and killed them—men, women, and children.[46]

Some say that the appearance of the cliffs from the sea is the source of the name **Hana-pēpē**, "crushed bay." However, others say the correct name is **Hana-pēpēhi**, "killing bay."[47] In addition, *hanapēpē* was the name given to a honeycreeper that is called *nukupu'u* on the other islands. It was notable for having one mandible much longer than the other. The name *hanapēpē* recalls the lost species of colorful birds whose feathers provided the raw materials of the finest form of Polynesian art—the feathered capes, helmets, standards, and wreaths. These lowland honeycreepers have all disappeared now, victims of an imported bird malaria and the loss of their forested habitat.

Wahiawa

Situated between Hanapēpē and Kalāheo, Wahi-awa *ahupua'a* begins at **Kāhili**, "feather standard," a 3,089-foot peak halfway up the ridge leading to Kawaikini and Wai'ale'ale. From its western side, the peak looks something like the tall feather standard for which it is named. The *kāhili* was a cylinder covered with feathers and attached to a long pole that always accompanied a chief or chiefess of high rank wherever they went.

At Kāhili, the boundaries of Kōloa, Hā'iku, Wahiawa, and Kalāheo *ahupua'a* all meet. Such a common border needed to be something recognizable, especially as this was birdcatching country. Like the laws that regulated the use of water, the laws concerning the *kia manu* (bird-catchers) were very strict. Each *ahupua'a* had to pay as tax a certain amount of feathers taken from the bright honeycreepers—the yellow of the *'anianiau*, the green of the *'ō'ū*, the red of the *olokele*. The *kia manu* always made sure that birds were left for breeding purposes. Some, like the black *'ō'ō 'ā'ā* that had only a few yellow feathers under its wings, were plucked and released to grow new ones. Many of the *kāhili* were decorated with the feathers of the *moa* (jungle fowl). The roosters have multicolored feathers, and the long tail plumes were ideal for display on a *kāhili*.

The ancients leveled off the top of Kāhili—an area twelve feet wide and twenty-seven feet long. Within this rectangle, several large tree trunks of the native *kauila* were set upright, each about twelve feet high. Notches were cut into each tree trunk as footholds. A remnant of a legend says these posts are part of a fort built by a chief who, on bad terms with his neighbors, decided to live here. The approaches to the fort are along narrow ridges, and these paths are easily defended. During the night the chief and his warriors would descend to the plains and bring back pigs, chickens, taro, and sweet potatoes for their sustenance. Neither the chief's name or his fate have survived.[48]

On the plains east of the valley itself is **Kāhili-na'i**, "conquering *kāhili*." Here, about 1700 A.D., two cousins fought a second time against each other. 'Aikanaka had been defeated by his cousin Kaweloleimakua and had lost his status as ruling chief of Kaua'i. Pretending he did not burn for vengeance, he befriended Kawelo's foster son and married his daughter to him. The foster son revealed that Kawelo did not know the arts and strategies of warfare using rocks as weapons. A warrior using a sling to launch water-polished rocks and men throwing coconut-sized rocks like a shot put could inflict deadly damage. 'Aikanaka mobilized the people of Wahiawa and Hanapēpē and built a wall along this plain by carrying up canoes and piling up rocks behind them. The plain was littered with rocks cast up by the last volcanic eruption in the area. Kawelo's brother, who lived in Waimea, heard about this, came to investigate, and was killed. After Kawelo arrived on the plain, he was brought down twice by stones, but he recovered himself to fight on. When he fell the third time, his body covered by rocks, Kawelo was declared dead. His body was wrapped in banana sheaves and carried to Maulili *heiau* in Kōloa to be sacrificed. 'Aikanaka raised Kawelo's conquered *kāhili* and declared himself once again the supreme ruler of the island.[49]

Wahi-awa means "milkfish place." *Awa,* the milkfish, was easily grown in taro fields, needing no other sustenance than the algae that grew among the taro corms. *Awa* was a source of protein and could be obtained whenever desired. A greatly appreciated relish was made of *awa* belly meat soaked in salted water and mixed with either *manauea,* a red seaweed, or *'o'olu,* a small red seaweed that melts in freshwater. Poki, a supernatural dog whose appearance usually announced some misfortune to the one who saw him, had his home in Wahiawa. Poki was noted for the exceptionally fat and tasty *awa* he grew in his taro fields.[50]

In the center of Wahiawa was a flat stone named **Kaua'i-iki,** "little Kaua'i," which is shaped like the island. Visitors who did not have time to make the journey around the island came here and walked around the stone. Then they could go home and boast, truthfully, that they had indeed walked around Kaua'i. When the present highway was being built, the rock was slated for destruction, but instead it was moved to Kukuiolono Park in Kalāheo. There a rushed visitor may still walk around Kaua'i in a moment.

Another Wahiawa rock preserved at Kukuiolono is **Pōhaku-loa,** "long rock." This tall, erect stone was once one of three in line, Pōhakuloa on the plain, one on the seacoast that is now gone, and one out in the sea where the deep-sea fishing grounds were. These stones together were a *ko'a* (fishing shrine) where a fisherman prayed for success on his way to fish and where he left an offering of the first catch of the day on his way home. Pōhakuloa was surrounded by a twelve-foot-wide pavement of smooth, flat, water-polished stones.[51]

Certain place-names suggest the richness of life in Wahiawa. **Ke-'uki-hōlua,** "sedge for a sled race course," was a land area of farms. *'Uki* is a sedge that grows in damp places and looks similar to a bulrush. These were used to cover a *hōlua* racecourse at the time of races, for they created a soft, slippery slide.

Nupa, "deep cave," was an *'ili* (a land division smaller than an *ahupua'a*). The name refers both to a particularly deep cave suitable for living and a purifying ceremony to insure growth or to clean contaminated persons—such as those who had handled corpses—or a prayer for the soul of one who had just died.

Ke-kualele, "flying god," was a poison god who was sent to destroy an enemy. Sometimes the spirit of a dead kinsman was fed with offerings and the need for his deadly mission explained. The *kualele* usually traveled in the form of fireballs.

At the top of the cliff overlooking the ocean is **Kani-mo'o-lae,** "headland of the singing dragon." What song was he or she singing, and why? Today Wahiawa is unpopulated, its stories forgotten.

Kalāheo

Ka-lā-heo, "proud day," begins at Kāhili peak and extends across the plains between Wahiawa on the west and Lāwa'i on the east. The *ahupua'a* is dominated by a huge cinder cone, **Kukui-o-Lono,** "light of Lono," and descends from there through a gulch to the sea at **Ka-wai-haka,** a name that refers to a shelf of water that gushes down the talus slopes into the sea. Kalāheo has a heavier rainfall than Wahiawa and is buffeted by the strong wind, **Ku'u-anu,** "releasing coldness."

Kukuiolono is visible from one end of Kona to the other, from Māhā'ulepū to Kekaha. A bonfire on this hill acted as a beacon for seafarers and was useful to all fishermen and travelers on the ocean south of the island.

At the top there was a large *heiau* that is now destroyed. It was built upon three terraces. The east section was 95 by 122 feet in dimension. The midsection was 105 by 83 feet, and the west division was 105 by 51 feet. On the seaward side the total length of this *heiau* was 246 feet. This made it the largest on the island.[52]

Its *'anu'u* (prayer tower) was three stories tall and covered with white *kapa* (tapa, bark cloth). It was the most sacred part of the temple. It also must have been visible from afar, adding to Kukuiolono's value as a guide for seafarers. The foundation of this *'anu'u* measures 22 by 30 feet, which indicates it was an unusually large tower.

Lono was one of the four major gods of the Hawaiians. He was god of clouds, winds, sea, fertility, and of agriculture. Therefore, any sacrifices of animals were done in a nearby *heiau*, **Ka-hale-ki'i**, "image house." It too was a three-terraced *heiau* of large size. The sacrificial altar on which the victims were killed was named **Nā-pōhaku-a-ki'i-ola**, "rocks of the living images." The offerings were brought dead to Kukuiolono so that Lono's altar would not be polluted with blood. Lono listened to prayers for rain, for abundant crops, and for escape from sickness or trouble.

Nearby was **Ipu-o-Lono**, "gourd of Lono," a small *heiau* that embodied the spiritual value of daily prayers. Each family owned an *ipuolono*, a food gourd covered with wickerwork and hung with strings from a notched stick. Vegetable food, fish, meat, and kava were kept in the gourd. Twice a day, the family head took the gourd down and laid it at the door of the house. Facing the sun, he prayed for his chief, his extended family, and for his own immediate family. Then he ate some of the food and sucked on the kava root. Afterward the *ipuolono* was washed, the food was replaced, and the gourd stored away again.[53]

On the seacoast is a deep pond, **Nō-milu**, "seepage whirls," and a series of salt pans that produced the finest and most desired salt of

NŌMILU

Kaua'i. People came in the summer to gather salt when the winds blew the salt across the surface of the pond to the edge of the pond, where it was carefully scooped out with the hands or with pieces of gourd shell and dried. The pond itself is about three hundred yards long by two hundred yards wide. There is a submarine connection with the sea, for the level of the pond rises and falls with the tide. Its depth varies from five to eleven fathoms. The name refers to water seeping away in the form of eddies or whirlpools.[54]

On one side of the pond is a spring called **Ka-kalua**, "sinkhole," where shrimp were caught. These shrimp were a light pink and had a white spot in front of the head and sometimes a white tail. The Menehune were especially fond of these shrimp, which are not always to be found here.

The site of the fishpond was once a small hill. Pele, before she

35

found her home in the volcano of Mauna Loa on Hawai'i, searched all of Kaua'i for a suitable place to live. When she came here, Nāmakaokaha'i caught up to her. Nāmakaokaha'i was Pele's older sister and greatest enemy. During the battle, Pele kicked up a lot of dirt into a pile, which turned into the hill **Kāpeku**, "to splash water by kicking the feet." Then Pele caused the hill she and her sister were fighting on to erupt, which covered the plains of Wahiawa with stones the size of coconuts. Nāmakaokaha'i flooded the new crater, forming the pond. Pele fled to O'ahu, followed by Nāmakaokaha'i. The cape at Nōmilu is named **Nā-maka-o-Kaha'i**, in memory of she who put out the volcano.

Before Pele left, she turned two supernatural eels, **Puhi-'ula**, "red eel," and **Puhi-pakapaka**, "scaly eel," into stone as guardians of the pond. They are still there.

Lāwa'i

Lāwa'i shares its border with Kalāheo and Kōloa beginning at **Ka-pōhā-kau**, "placed rock," a 1,400-foot-high peak on the ridge below Kāhili. Its headwaters do not reach into the rainy swampland at the top of the island. Both boundaries follow from hilltop to hilltop, reaching the shore of low, black lava cliffs broken by a small crescent bay.

The demigod Poki owned land in Lāwa'i. Poki appeared in the guise either of a large black dog or as a small white dog, depending on his mission. Poki is thought to be a manifestation of Kū-'īlio-loa, whose cloud form is often seen stretched out on the mountains. Kū was the first of the four major Polynesian gods to arrive on Kaua'i. He was the god of rain and war and could be either beneficial or cruel. He often chose to appear in dog form.[55]

There was a fishing shrine on the cliffs to the east of the bay. Below its ruins there is a round, smooth bowl carved in the rocks just above the sea. It is about nine inches across and resembles the mouth of a fish. Priests prepared 'awa and poured it into this hole as an offering

PUHI

to the shark god, Kū-haimoana. He was the largest of the shark gods, a male whose mouth was said to be as big as an ordinary grass house and enabled him to swallow two or three common sharks with ease. He was so huge that he could not live in the channels around O'ahu and Maui and so resided in the deep waters off the island of Ka'ula. When the offering was made, Kūhaimoana rode the breakers to the base of the cliff and drank from the bowl. Only then would fishermen leave the shore for the deep-sea fishing grounds.[56]

In the middle of the stream, near the mouth, lies a rock. This is the body of Hina, a woman who was ardently pursued by a man she did not wish as a lover. In order to escape him she jumped into the river, where he turned her into stone. The long stone is completely covered by water and is overgrown with moss. In olden times women came to Hina, stood on her back, and prayed for her help to soothe the path of their romantic desires. Hina, unlucky in her own love life, always helped them.[57]

At the river mouth is **Kai-ho'olale**, "encouraging the sea," a small island of twenty-foot-high cliffs. There was a fishpond tucked in behind it that was washed out in the great flood of 1846.

The most famous landmark of Lāwa'i is **Puhi**, "eel," the Spouting Horn. Within a leaf of black lava jutting into the ocean there is a large hole that opens into the sea. When a wave surges against the lava leaf, water rushes through the hole and erupts as a geyser with a mighty roar. The spume rises thirty or more feet, then subsides to await the next large wave. It is a spectacular sight with a frightening sound and, as one might expect, there is more than one story to account for it.

Kai-kapu, a *mo'o* (water dragon) with a ferocious appetite and bad temper, would hide behind a nearby point. Swimming furiously and roaring loudly, she would scoop up anyone foolish enough to fish along the shore. Soon the shoreline became deserted. Once a young boy, Liko, wanted to catch *hīnālea* (wrasse) for his grandmother. He got his traps and other gear and jumped into the water. Immediately

Kaikapu came rushing toward him and Liko, being small, swam into a lava tube that opened onto land from the sea. Kaikapu plunged after him, but she was so large that she became permanently stuck in the lava tube. The roaring one hears as the ocean flows through the tube are the roars of frustrated and angry Kaikapu.[58]

Another story says the sound is not a roar of anger but a moan of grief. Long, long ago there were two sisters and a brother who lived in Tahiti. Their other siblings had many children who crawled over these three until they were very tired of it. So they decided to assume the forms of giant eels and travel to another place where they would not be constantly disturbed. When they finally reached Niʻihau, the two sisters were so tired that they went ashore to rest, but the brother went on to investigate Kauaʻi. After many years the brother became lonely for the company of his sisters and returned to Niʻihau. He found that his sisters had fallen asleep in the sun and had been baked into solid rock; they can still be seen. He wept bitterly over them and, returning to Kauaʻi blinded by tears, he blundered into the lava tube and became stuck fast. The roaring sounds one hears are the sobs of the brother as he still cries for his sisters.[59]

Kōloa

Ka-uhu-ʻula, "red parrotfish," is a ridge that descends from Kāhili peak onto the plains that mark the beginning of the Puna District. At the bottom is the area called Ka-moʻo-loa, "long ridge," the scene of many battles. Here Palila was born during the period of war between the kingdoms of Puna and Kona about 1200 A.D. He was raised by his grandmother in the *heiau* of ʻĀlana-pō, "night offering," sacred to the gods from the time of darkness. Palila, named after a honeycreeper that lives only on the island of Hawaiʻi, was trained in all the warfare skills by the gods. His father was Ka-lua-o-pālena and his mother was Mahi-nui. Palila saved his father from defeat at the hands of the Kona leader by wielding a huge war club so expertly that it filled the opposing army with crippling fear. Palila got his great strength by eating only bananas that were grown especially for him in two renowned patches. Eventually, Palila became the *aliʻi nui* of Hilo on the island of Hawaiʻi.[60]

On the plains of Kamoʻoloa is a small stream called **Weoweo-pilau,** "rotten bigeye fish." It seems an upland farmer heard that the bigeye fish were running at the beach, so he went down and caught a great number of them. On his way home, an old woman asked him for a few fish but he refused to give her any, saying she could go to the shore and get as many as she wanted. As he continued home, his load of fish became heavier and heavier, the path dustier and dustier, and the sun blazed with heat. When he reached this stream, he put down his fish and plunged in to cool off. When he came out, he smelled that his fish were completely rotten. He then realized that the old lady had been Pele, the volcano goddess, testing his generosity and hospitality. He had been found wanting and was punished.[61]

The *ahupuaʻa* is well watered by constantly flowing streams. Two of these, the ʻŌmaʻo, "green," and Pō-ʻeleʻele, "dark night," feed the area of Pīwai (a variety of wild duck). Where they join, the stream becomes **Wai-komo,** "entering water," which flows down the center of the land, bringing life to the drier regions toward the seashore. It is so named because from time to time the stream disappears for a bit before reappearing farther down the slope.

There is a deep pool in Waikomo Stream, toward the center of the *ahupuaʻa,* called **Mau-lili,** "constant jealousy." On the eastern bank of the pool sits a rock called **Wai-hānau,** "birth pool." Below Waihānau was a rock shaped something like a human tongue called **Ka-ʻōlelo-o-Hawaiʻi,** "language of Hawaiʻi." It is said that Kaweloleimakua, who lived at the end of the 1600s, brought this rock to Kauaʻi from the island of Hawaiʻi.[62] Kiha-wahine, the fearsome *moʻo* goddess, lived in this pool. When she was in residence, the water turned red and no one dared to swim there.

When the gods Kāne and Kanaloa first came to Kaua'i, they explored the island. They came to Maulili at evening and stretched out beside the pool for their night's sleep. When they arose the next morning, the imprint of their bodies was left behind and could be pointed out even into this century.

Maulili is also the name of Kōloa's most important *heiau*. It was first built by Ka-pueo-maka-walu, the son of Kapu-lau-kī. He had his house on the eastern side of this *heiau*. It was a place of human sacrifice, but once Kapueomakawalu died, it was no longer used and its location was lost.[63]

Many years later, when 'Aikanaka had overcome his cousin Kawelo in the battle of stones on the plains of Wahiawa, 'Aikanaka wanted a place to sacrifice the body. He asked that the location of Maulili be found, but no one knew anything about it. At last, a deaf mute was asked and he knew. He led 'Aikanaka to the place, pointed out the remains of the stone walls, and the *heiau* was rebuilt.[64]

'Aikanaka built a house on the northeastern side where he spent one night. In the morning, he went to Maulili to offer the body of Kawelo to the gods. Instead he found that Kawelo had revived from the wounds he had received, and thus it was 'Aikanaka who became the sacrifice on the altar that day.[65]

Kapueomakawalu also built the *heiau* of Louma, which stood on the mountain side of Ho'oleina-ka-pua'a, "place to throw in the pig." This was beside a small pond *mauka* of Maulili. Louma was a small *heiau* in which hogs, red fishes, and other sacrifices were offered. It was dedicated to Lono-i-ka-ou-ali'i, the god who had come to Kaua'i with La'a-mai-kahiki in the twelfth century. The stones for this *heiau* were brought from O'ahu. It is said that the Menehune did the actual building.[66]

The sea shore was lined with shrines. **Manini,** "surgeonfish," was dedicated to Kūhaimoana, the ferocious shark god. On the night of Kāne in every month, a drum was beaten to proclaim a *kapu*. No one was allowed to go to the beach on those nights for fear they might step on one of the shark gods. On those nights, the twenty-seventh in the lunar cycle, Kūhaimoana and other shark gods came up to the beach and took spiritual possession of their keepers. Anyone foolish enough to break the *kapu* became a meal for the sharks.[67]

Hālau-a-ka-lena, "shed for the *'olena,* turmeric plant," was dedicated to the dreaded dragon goddess Kihawahine. If she was offended she would take the form of a sea dragon and patrol the seashore, killing all who dared fish from canoes and along the reef and rocks.[68]

Hana-kā'ape, "headstrong bay," is a small bay once used as an anchorage by whaling ships wintering in the islands before returning to the hunt in the cold northern seas. At this place, Kapo-'ula-kina'u, sister of the volcano goddess Pele, first took spiritual possession of another person. As Kapo and her companions were coming down the path to Hana-kā'ape, Kapo saw a man running to a house where a woman was weaving a mat. The man struck the woman with his fist. The woman cried out as he hit her again and again. Kapo had seen no reason for his anger, and the punishment being inflicted on the woman filled her with rage.

Kapo changed the woman into a reddish brown dog. The dog turned on the man and bit him, trying to tear out his throat. His neighbors came rushing to his help but there was nothing they could do to save him. As the man died, Kapo whistled for the dog and it ran directly to her. Kapo took a piece of *mahiki* grass and put it into the dog's mouth. It vanished and the woman stood before Kapo.

The neighbors rushed at the woman to kill her but Kapo, in her wind form, entered the woman and made her behave as though she were mentally deranged. It was believed that craziness was caused by an *'aumakua* (a family god or guardian) and that such a person was favored by the gods; thus, such people were left strictly alone. The woman began to chant, calling her neighbors by name and predicting their near future. Many of these predictions came true, and from then on whenever this woman chanted, her neighbors listened very carefully. Certainly their husbands knew better than to beat their wives.[69]

There are three possible meanings of the name **Kōloa**. First, the land may have been named after the *koloa maoli*, a native duck that lived in the large marshes that covered much of the western area of the *ahupuaʻa*. Two migratory ducks once found in this area at certain times of the year are the *koloa mapu*, the pin-tailed duck, and the *koloa moha*, the shoveler or spoonbill duck. The indigenous *koloa maoli* is not a migratory bird and it has been considered an endangered species since 1978.

It is also said that the *ahupuaʻa* took its name from a steep rock on the east bank of Maulili Pond in Waikomo Stream. The rock is named **Pali-o-Koloa**, "cliff of Koloa," but there is no indication of who or what Koloa was.

The name may also be **Kō-loa**, "tall sugarcane." Sugarcane was one of the plants brought by the original Polynesian settlers and grown in gardens and along the banks of taro patches as a source of sugar. Sometimes the leaves were used for thatching houses. Kauaʻi farmers had names for at least forty varieties of sugarcane, and the tallest *kō* grew up to thirty feet in height. It was perhaps no accident that Hawaiʻi's first sugar plantation was established at Kōloa.[70]

Weliweli

The former kingdom and present district of Kona ends in three small *ahupuaʻa*, sun-baked and dry, lying between the reef-lined shore and the Hāʻupu ridge that deprives them of rain.

Weliweli, "fearful," still has remnants of rough stone-walled enclosures whose construction bears a great similarity to those built in Kalalau, but nowhere else.[71] When the island was being explored by the Menehune, who had been brought to Kauaʻi by Kūʻalunuipaukūmokumoku, one adventuresome group was led by

Weliweli, a gruff-voiced man. He was very strict and everyone jumped to fulfill his orders. This area was named after him.[72]

Its east boundary begins at the headland **Maka-hūena**, "eyes over-flowing with heat." Sometimes the headland shimmers in the summer sun, and whenever that happened it was believed that a procession of departed chiefs and their followers were on the move. It was safest to stay away until the shimmering stopped.[73]

At the upper end of this *ahupua'a* was a swamp that now has been dammed to create a reservoir for the sugar plantation. At one time this area was covered by forest. Palila, son of Ka-lua-o-pā-lena, left the *heiau* where he had been raised and trained, curious about the noise of battle he heard. He climbed to the peak **Kū-manumanu**, "scarred Kū," and looked down on the battlefield. He saw his father's army on one side and the Kona enemy led by Nā-maka-o-ka-lani on the other, seemingly ready for the usual face-to-face battle. However, Palila noted that, unknown to his father, the enemy chief had concealed many of his warriors in the woods. Palila took his war club and with one sweep felled a tree at the edge of this forest. It fell against its neighbor with such force that the neighbor fell too, and one by one all the trees in the forest toppled, crushing the enemy beneath them.

Then Palila rested his war club on the ground. It was so heavy that it sank deep into the ground. When Palila pulled it out, a gush of water welled out. This spring, **Wai-hohonu**, "deep water," covered the once mighty forest, creating the swamp of **Pālena**, named after Palila's father.[74]

Wai-hohonu is sometimes given as **Wai-o-honu**, "stream of the tur-tle," and the giant stone turtle on the ridge above is pointed out as being the turtle in question. A female turtle dug out a hole for a nest, but a never-ending gush of water greeted her. On her way to search for another nesting site, she was turned to stone.[75]

Another explanation for the swamp tells of a maiden who lived at Palena, her house surrounded by a fence of *'ōlena* plants. Her lover used to come from his home down the coast by canoe and walk up to visit. He became irritated that she was never ready to receive him, there was no food prepared, the house was not neat, and so on. She retorted that since the forest obstructed her view and he never sent a messenger to announce his coming, there was no way she could anticipate his coming. The young man seized an ax and cut down all the trees, giving the young woman a clear view over the plains to the sea and plenty of time to have things ready for his arrival.[76]

Pāʻā

This dry, arid *ahupuaʻa* contains 3,263 acres. A stone wall, Pā-ʻā, "fence of lava rock," marked the boundary between it and Weliweli to the foot of the ridge **Ka-lae-o-ka-honu**, "headland of the turtle." The border continues up the ridge to **Ka-maʻu-lele**,[77] a peak of 1,509 feet in the Hāʻupu Range. The seafront is dominated by a crescent beach called **Ke-one-loa**, "long beach," where there were *kuakua paʻakai* (salt ponds).[78] There is an extensive petroglyph field here, the largest field of these carvings on the island. There have been only four recorded sightings: 1848, 1887, 1897, and 1916. This area has been bulldozed to make room for a hotel and a golf course complex.

On the headland between Pāʻā and Weliweli stood a large *heiau*, **Kāne-ʻaukai**, "seafaring man." Kāneʻaukai was the oldest brother of Maikoha, who at his death turned into the hairy *wauke* (paper mulberry). Four of his sisters were transformed into fishing grounds, each attracting a different species of fish. His body was in the shape of a log of wood that drifted ashore here and was carried in and out by the tide for several days. Tiring of this, Kāneʻaukai changed into his human form and came ashore. He came across two old men fishing. From time to time they would chant a prayer, but as the prayer was not directed to any god in particular it was caught by the wind and blown away. Kāneʻaukai asked them why they did not pray to a particular fishing god; they replied that although they knew of a god who could help them, they did not know his name. Kāne'aukai replied: "His name is Kāne-'aukai, and when you let down your nets again call out, *'Eia ka 'ai a me ka i'a, e Kāne'aukai,'* 'Here is the food and fish, Kane-'aukai,' and he will help you." The old men followed his instructions, and each time they threw in their nets they drew up a great haul of fish. Other people heard of the old men's great success in fishing and came to learn the name of the fishing god, too.[79]

Pā'ā was noted for its *he'e* (octopus), which were particularly large and delicious. It was the favorite food of Ke-akia-niho, the *konohiki* who had become the local chief after Kaluaopālena, with the help of his son Palila, had conquered Nāmakaokalani of Kona, and he looked forward happily to a lifetime supply of his favorite food. Within weeks, however, the *he'e* of Pā'ā disappeared. Keakianiho sent for his *kahuna* Kāne-a-ka-lua to discover the reason for this lack. The priest hid on the ridge above and soon saw a giant crab with eleven dark red spots on its back emerge from a hole in the ground and enter the ocean. After a time it returned, bearing *he'e* in its claws, and disappeared into the hole.

When the *konohiki* and his soldiers found the hole, they saw that it led underground into a network of large caves where they found a handful of defeated Kona warriors and a fierce battle took place. At the end, none of the enemy survived. The caves were searched for the large crab, but it was never seen again. Shortly thereafter, however, the reef of Pā'ā became filled with little *'alamuku* crabs, each bearing eleven red spots on its back.[80]

Māhā'ulepū

The boundary of Māhā'ulepū follows the Pā'ā border to Kuma'ulele peak and then continues along the ridge to the top of Hā'upu mountain, then goes down the western ridge named **Lae-ka-weli-koa**, "point of the warrior's terror," to the sea. The *ahupua'a* is only 1,572 acres in size.

On the border with Pā'ā is the *heiau* of **Wai-o-pili**, "water of the *pili* grass." Beside it is a spring, **Ka-puna-kea**, "white spring," which feeds the pond of Waiopili. It is the major source of fresh water in Māhāʻulepū. The clear water looks white because of the limestone background. The pond is also the habitat of a rare blind shrimp that was used in religious ceremonies.[81]

The name **Mā-hā'ule-pū**, "and falling together," refers to the great sea and land battle that took place here during the 1300s when Ka-lau-nui-o-Hua of Hawaiʻi attempted to become ruler of all of the islands. He had conquered the ruling chiefs of Maui, Molokaʻi, and Oʻahu, and with them as prisoners set sail for Kauaʻi. Kauaʻi's ruling chief, Kūkona, knew they were coming and hid his army in the ridges above and withdrew all his canoes into Hanapēpē Bay. He allowed Kalaunuiohua to land unopposed and soon the Hawaiʻi canoes were drawn up on the beach, the royal prisoners safely housed, and all the invading warriors formed into their fighting order. Then Kūkona, dressed in full royal regalia of helmet and cloak and with his *kāhili* towering above him, appeared on the ridge above. Kalaunuiohua hurried to meet his enemy, but when he arrived, no chief was there. Then a shout was heard, and Kalaunuiohua saw Kūkona on the neighboring ridge. From ridge to ridge, Kūkona drew his invaders farther and farther from the beach, until they reached the plains of Wahiawa. Here Kūkona ordered his army to attack, and the invading army, stretched thinly over so many miles, was easily defeated.

Meanwhile, Kūkona's canoe fleet sped from Hanapēpē and caught the fleet of invading canoes before they had even had time to launch them again. In the fierce battle between canoes, blood flowed freely. Only one enemy canoe managed to escape to bring the dreadful news back to their home island. By nightfall, Kalaunuiohua's army was gone and he was a prisoner. The other royal prisoners had been found, and Kūkona thus found himself in the position of being able to take command of all the islands. While he decided what to do, he took his captured chiefs on an extended tour of the island.[82]

The ridge under which the canoe fleet had been destroyed was called **Ka-weli-koa**, "terror of the warriors," and the cape where the canoes had come ashore became **Nā-'ākea**, "starboard hulls of a double canoe." The bay became **Papa-mō'ī**, "platform of the king," in memory of the five ruling chiefs who met here.

No people who love puns as much as the Polynesians could resist playing with the name Mā-hā'ule-pū. A subtle change creates **Maha-'ule-pu**, "inactive foreskin," said as a complaint by the wives of the men who spent all their time throwing fishing nets off the reefs until their hands, feet, and other appendages become too waterlogged and shriveled to be used.[83]

Puna District

Napali

Halele'a

Ko'olau

West Kona

East Kona

*T*he ancient kingdom of Puna lies between the walls of Wai‘ale‘ale and the sea, cradled by the arms of the Hā‘upu Range on the south and the Makaleha Mountains to the north. This area is watered by three small rivers—Hulē‘ia, Hanamā‘ulu, and Ke‘ālia—that fed complexes of taro fields. The center of the land was and is dominated by the watershed of the mighty Wailua River. It begins in the countless waterfalls that cascade down an immense green amphitheater formed by three-thousand-foot cliffs. Small tributaries join to form larger ones and these combine into two large streams, the North and South Forks, which together cut a path through the ridge lying crossways inland of the shore. The river becomes broad, deep, and slow, Hawai‘i's longest navigable stream. It was the center of Kaua‘i's second kingdom, Puna.

For six to eight hundred years, from the time of Kū‘alunuikiniākua, the inhabitants of Kona centered on the Waimea River had little or no contact with the islands to the south. The population peacefully grew and expanded into new areas, developing new homes, agricultural fields, and temples.

Then sometime between 1000 and 1100 A.D., settlers from the Marquesas arrived, led by Puna-nui-ka-ia-‘āina. There is no trace in surviving legends of the negotiations that must have taken place to accomodate these new settlers, but Punanuikaia‘āina succeeded in creating a chiefdom independent of Kona.[1]

The Puna kingdom grew to accommodate an increasing population and spread out on both sides of the river until it covered the area between the Hā‘upu Range and the Makaleha Mountains. By the end of the fourteenth century, seven *ahupua‘a* were created to the south and five to the north of the river.

Ha‘ikū

Because each *ahupua‘a* needed access to the sea, Ha‘ikū has an unusual shape. At the eastern end, it includes the mountain range that overhangs Nāwiliwili Harbor, a narrow strip along the Hulē'ia River, and then it bulges out in the upland flats, touching the Kona District in the gap between two mountain ranges. Ha'ikū can be translated in several different ways: "to speak abruptly," "haughty," "conceited," or "sharp break."

The story of its naming is lost and a new story has taken its place. This story says Ha'ikū also means "pushed through," recalling that the volcano goddess Pele and the demigod Kamapua'a first met in Ha'ikū. Kamapua'a was smitten with Pele's beauty, but when she refused his advances he tried to rape her. She was saved by her sister Kapo'ulakīna'u who sent her detachable vagina to entice Kamapua'a, which it did. Pele and Kamapua'a eventually married and had a son, but their relationship was always stormy and angry and did not last.[2]

The headland pointing farthest into the sea is Ka-lani-pu'u, "royal hill" or "heavenly hill." It is 779 feet high and was formerly a pu'u kāhea (calling hill), where the head fisherman called out his instructions to fishermen in their canoes. Pele's sister, Nāmakaokaha'i, planted 'awa and bananas here. 'Awa root, chewed, watered, and strained, makes a narcotic drink much prized throughout Polynesia. It is bitter tasting and is usually followed by some relish, often a bite of banana, to sweeten the mouth.[3]

An 'ili (a land division smaller than an ahupua'a) and an irrigation ditch were named Kua-'ā, "burning back."[4] This was the name of a severe taboo on approaching a chief from behind. Anyone except the chief's closest servants going behind a chief meant instant death. The Kaua'i executioners, called mū, were experts at the art of strangulation. Chiefs or chiefesses with this taboo could not lend any bit of clothing that had touched their back, nor was anyone permitted to touch them unless elaborate ceremonies had been conducted by a kahuna nui to free the kapu.

Near the northern end of the Hā'upu Range, the ridge has a deep straight-sided cut which is called Ka-ho'olei-nā-pe'a, "to fly kites." In the late 1600s, 'Aikanaka and his twin brother were born in the *heiau* of Holoholokū. Two other boys had been born there the same night: Kaweloleimakua and Kauahoa. Kauahoa was extremely large and had a fierce loyalty to 'Aikanaka. Kawelo, on the other hand, was small but full of pride, ambition, and mischievousness. He delighted in playing tricks on 'Aikanaka. The only person he feared was Kauahoa, and he constantly challenged him to any sort of contest hoping to learn how Kauahoa's superior size could be overcome. Once Kawelo challenged Kauahoa to a kite-flying contest. Both boys built their own kites and launched them. Kauahoa's soared high—so high Kawelo knew his could not do as well. Maneuvering his kite string, Kawelo caused his kite to tangle with Kauahoa's and break the strings. The two kites flew free and crashed into the Hā'upu ridge, leaving a sharply defined vee shape still easily seen from the highway. Kauahoa did not challenge Kawelo or fight him, as Kawelo would surely have done, and in that moment Kawelo lost his fear of Kauahoa and knew he could beat him in any future contest.[5]

The Hā'upu Range ends at a hill 642 feet high named **Ka-hoa-ea**, "coming up of the companion." Long ago a chief named 'Olopana lived in Wailua. He had a daughter named Lu'ukia and when he heard that his brother, who lived in Hilo, had a son, 'Olopana swore that Lu'ukia would marry no one else but this nephew of his. The boy was named 'Uwe'uwele-kēhau. When he became a man he traveled alone to Kaua'i to meet this woman whom he had to marry. They were immediately attracted to each other and decided to marry. 'Olopana became very angry. After all, the young man had not openly announced his arrival in the usual chiefly manner—sailing on a red-sailed canoe, a feather cape across his shoulders and a red *malo* around his waist. 'Olopana, thinking the man a nobody, banished the young couple, taking away all their possessions including their clothes, and told his people not to take these two into their homes nor give them food or clothing. He sent them to Mānā, which at that time was only a place of spirits where no people lived. Lu'ukia and Uwe'uwelekēhau left Wailua and began to walk to Mānā. As they crested the top of Kilohana Crater, Lu'ukia began to cry. She saw that people were following them and she was ashamed of being naked; besides, she was hungry. Her husband pointed to the hill in front of them where he could see a group waiting for their arrival and said, "Be patient until we reach that hill over there." When they got to the foot of the hill, there was indeed food and clothing waiting for them. The people who had been following them now caught up to Uwe'uwelekēhau and Lu'ukia and said they intended to share their exile.[6]

Kīpū

One definition of **Kīpū** is "to remain, as mist or rain," an apt name for this area. Hā'upu is often capped with a cloud that floats like a great white bird. This cloud was called Ke-ao-lewa, "clouds of the atmosphere." Sometimes the peak is surrounded by puffy clouds called "pig clouds,"—one of the forms of Kamapua'a. Whenever these clouds are seen, it is a clear sign of coming rain.

Kīpū straddles the Hā'upu Range, which cuts the *ahupua'a* in two. **Kīpū-uka**, "upland Kīpū," on the north side is a lush, wet land now used as a cattle ranch. **Kīpū-kai**, "Kīpū at the sea," on the south side is a dry, rounded valley bordered by miles of white sand beach. Kīpūkai had a fish pond and salt ponds. There were house sites and walls on the lower part of the ridge, as well as burial sites in the dunes along the shore. Gourds, yams, and sweet potatoes grew well here. A rock, **Pōhā-kua**, "rock ridge," on the seashore has a petroglyph on it.

The sea yielded conch shells in profusion, as indicated by five Kīpūkai names: **Ka-pū-ali'i**, "chief's conch shell"; **Pū-hoihoi**, "joyful conch shell"; **Pū-hua**, "prolific conch shell"; **Pū-hui**, "cluster of triton shells"; and **Pū-aku**, "conch shell colored like a bonito."

Hana-nena, "bay of the *nena* plant," is the bay between **Kua-honu**, "turtle back," and **Lae-ka-weli-koa**, "point of the terror of warriors."

The *nena* was also called *kīpūkai*. It is the indigenous seaside heliotrope, a low perennial herb twelve to twenty-four inches long with narrow, hoary leaves and white or pale purple flowers. *Nena* was dried, brewed for tea, and used as a tonic.[7]

Two rocks associated with the demigod Kamapua'a are here. The first has a hole in which there is a cylindrical rock of such shape that it cannot be pulled out of the larger rock. Kamapua'a spied on two chiefesses bathing in a pool. He grew so excited that he thrust his hog's corkscrew-shaped penis into the convenient hole in the rock, but it broke off and remains lodged in the hole. Being a demigod, he was able to grow a new one.[8]

The other rock is a huge boulder as large as a room that is kept from rolling downhill by a small rock wedged under it. Two chiefesses saw a large black pig asleep and rolled the huge rock down to crush it. The pig was Kamapua'a. Hearing the noise of the tumbling rock, he woke up, realized his danger, and changed into his human form. He picked up a rock and threw it so that it wedged under the boulder, stopping its movement. Kamapua'a was so handsome that the chiefesses, who were sisters, married him. These chiefesses were guardians of Ke-mamo Spring. Their father Kāne-iki was engaged in constant battles against the Kona forces and many times came close to losing. The chiefesses grew angry with their husband for he only slept all day and never went down to the battlefield to fight alongside Kāneiki. Unknown to them, Kamapua'a could make himself invisible and in this guise went daily to the battlefield to fight. All the opposing warriors could see was a hand wielding a huge warclub, and it caused much panic. One day, a warrior managed to hit the hand and caused the thumb to bleed. This was reported to Kāneiki, who was extremely curious as to who this unknown and invisible warrior was. He also wondered why all the feather capes and helmets worn by the fallen enemy, which were by rights his, had never been found on the battlefield. Kāneiki called all his men together to find the unknown warrior, but no one was injured on the thumb. It was noticed that his son-in-law was not present, and Kāneiki went to find him.

Meanwhile, the sisters were so angry at Kamapua'a that when he asked for water they refused to bring him any and hid Kemamo Spring so that he could not find it. Turning into a cloud, Kamapua'a rose to the top of Hā'upu and, looking down, could see the spring clearly. Reverting to his pig form, Kamapua'a rooted up the spring, drank his fill, and turned the sisters into the rocks that still guard Kemamo, **Kukui-lau-mānienie**, "barren leafed candlenut tree," and **Kukui-lau-hanahana**, "smelly leafed candlenut tree."[9]

Nearby there is another spring called **Wai-'au'au-o-Hi'iaka**, "bathing water of Hi'iaka." When Pele first arrived on Kaua'i, she created a spring here where her youngest sister Hi'iaka-i-ka-poli-o-Pele could wash the salt from her skin. Later, traveling in her spirit form, Pele looked for this spring, but she could not find it. The two chiefesses, wives of Kamapua'a, had hidden it. They taunted Pele but the volcano goddess, although furious, could do nothing about it and left.[10]

The mountain range is dominated by Hā'upu, a 2,297-foot peak. The name means "recollection," but the story of its naming is lost. There is, however, a story of Hā'upu, a giant who lived on top of this mountain. Hā'upu was very large and very nervous, reacting violently to every sound. He did so much damage unwittingly and was so contrite afterwards he became even more nervous. So his *ali'i nui* sent him to the mountain to keep watch over the ocean and to warn if any invading fleet of canoes was on the way. Hā'upu never slept very much for fear he would miss a canoe fleet. One night he was awakened from a doze by the sounds of shouting. Looking toward O'ahu, Hā'upu saw lights flickering on the horizon. Convinced an invasion was coming, Hā'upu threw some huge stones he had gathered toward the invaders. The lights went out, the voices died away, and Hā'upu went back to sleep. A few days later, a messenger reported that O'ahu was in great sorrow. The chief of Wai'anae had gathered his people together at Ka'ena point for a great fishing festival. They had taken their canoes out to lay nets by torchlight. People on shore, also with torches, gathered fish from the reef, calling out to each other, chanting and laughing. Suddenly huge stones had fallen from the sky, one smashing the fleet of canoes, another falling atop the reef. Many people had been killed, including the chief. One of the rocks is still there and is called Pōhaku-o-Kaua'i, "rock of Kaua'i."[11]

On the side of Hā'upu, there is the profile of a woman with her finger poised in warning before her lips. Long ago Pele'ula, an O'ahu chiefess, kept hearing reports of the beauty of Kaua'i women. This made her curious, for her own court was noted for the loveliness of its women. She voyaged to Kaua'i to visit Hina, her counterpart on the island. Hina held a great feast, inviting all the ali'i to meet her guest. Among those who came was Kāhili, a young, tall, handsome chief who immediately attracted the attention of the two chiefesses. They decided to hold a contest. Each woman would dress herself in her most beautiful clothing and would dance a hula. The young chief was to be both judge and prize. Pele'ula adorned herself with wreaths of yellow 'ilima. She danced before the assemblage and sat down, well pleased with her efforts and with the effect she had had on the chief. Then Hina rose, dressed in kapa in which mokihana had been beaten and decked with wreaths of intertwined maile and mokihana. The perfume filled the room as Hina danced, and no one was more delighted to announce her loss than Pele'ula herself. "Kaua'i women are the most beautiful," she exclaimed. "You must warn future visitors!" So Hina's profile, Hina-i-uka, was carved on the mountain slope and her finger warns that indeed, Kaua'i's beauties are beyond compare.[12]

This rock face has become known as Queen Victoria's Profile. The former Queen of England is seen wagging her finger at her wayward son and saying, "Now, Willy! Willy!"—a pun based on the fact that she is facing Nāwiliwili Bay.[13]

Niumalu

Sharing modern Nāwiliwili Harbor is the *ahupuaʻa* of **Niu-malu,** "shaded coconut trees." After many adventures on other islands, Kapūnohu traveled to Waimea to begin a tour of Kauaʻi. When he reached Kōloa, he was warned to turn back as there was a man named Kemamo who lived on the border between Kona and Puna. He challenged all travelers to a contest. Kemamo was very skillful in the use of the sling. It was said he never missed a shot and that rocks flung from his sling could go as far as five miles. Kapūnohu continued his journey and was met by Kemamo. The two settled the terms of their bet, Kemamo's sling against Kapūnohu's spear thrown toward Kalalea peak, which was visible from where they were. Kemamo took up his sling and threw his stone. It flew across the uplands of Puna and dropped down near Anahola. Kapūnohu threw his spear. As it flew, it shaded the coconut trees, thus the name Niumalu, dipped into the Wailua River, hence the name Waiehu, and finally pierced the mountain at Kalalea leaving a large hole that was visible until just a few years ago.[14]

In Niumalu there is a large fishpond now called the **Menehune Fishpond.** The dam for this pond was built across a large bend in the Hulēʻia River and is a nine-hundred-yard dirt levee faced with stone. The rocks used for the facing, the story goes, came from the plains of Wahiawa and were passed from hand to hand down a double row of men and women. The pond was built at the request of Chief ʻAlekoko and Chiefess Ka-lālā-lehua, who were brother and sister. The Menehune insisted that these two must remain inside their house and must not peek out at the work in progress. Through the long night and most of the day, the two listened to the voices of the Menehune and heard the sounds of stone falling on stone. At last curiosity won out, and the brother poked his fingers through the grass thatch of the house and peered out. Immediately the Menehune chief ordered his people

'ALEKOKO

to drop the stones they were holding and wash their hands in the almost completed fishpond. The rocks were not water polished and there was not a hand that wasn't bleeding from several cuts. The Menehune left the dam unfinished as a reminder to Chief 'Alekoko of his broken promise. The fishpond still bears his name: 'Ale-koko, "rippling blood."[15]

Nāwiliwili

Nāwiliwili was famous for its grove of *wiliwili* trees. The *wiliwili* is a member of the legume family and has pealike flowers that are clustered near the ends of the branches ranging in color from red, orange, yellow to white. The pods have bright red seeds which are used to make bead necklaces.

The full name of this *ahupua'a* was Nā-wiliwili-paka-'āwili-lau-'ili-lua, "*wiliwili* trees upon which raindrops fall, twisting the leaves so the rain touches both sides."

One of the oldest *heiau* on the island was **Kuhi-au**, "I gesture," which was located at the site of the present Līhuʻe High School. It was in continual use, unlike most of the others that were refurbished only when there was a need. Kuhiau was a large, paved *heiau* that covered an area of about four acres. Even today, it is said that one can hear the drums beating at night and see the *akua lele* (flying gods) in the form of flashing lights.[16] On the reef was a rock, **Pua-kini**, "multitude of flowers," where the *kahuna nui* of Kuhiau lived. The rock and the reef were covered over with dirt to create the modern port, but Puakini can be seen in old photographs.

Farther upland is the modern town of **Lī-huʻe**, "goose flesh." Governor Ka-iki-o-ʻEwa, who was the first governor of Kauaʻi under the Kamehameha conquerors, named his home, which he built in 1825, in memory of his earlier home town on Oʻahu. The name was unknown on the island before then. The ancient name for this area was **Ka-laʻi-a-mea**, "calm reddish brown place."[17]

Another village of both modern and ancient times is **Puhi**, "blow," "set on fire," or "eel." As a shark god, Ka-holi-o-Kāne lived in a cave here. He was a shark god of Ka-lani-ʻōpuʻu, a chief under Kamehameha I who ordered the wholesale killing of Kauaʻi *aliʻi* after their ill-fated rebellion in 1824. With Kua, a shark god of Kohala, Ka-holi-o-Kāne raised a storm between Kauaʻi and Oʻahu to destroy Hiʻiaka in order to prevent the marriage of their relative Pele with Lohiʻau. Hiʻiaka overcame the storm, found Lohiʻau, and returned to Hawaiʻi.[18]

Kalapakī

The *ahupuaʻa* of **Kalapakī**, "double-yolked egg," is very small and is fronted by a crescent beach. There must have been an incident connected with an egg that has been long forgotten.

Ninini, "to pour," is a small sand beach and a point of land where the cliff stands straight up from the ocean and a *heiau* once stood. The name comes from the favorite pastime of the Menehune. They carried small stones with them from their mountain homes when they went to swim and placed these stones in heaps on the top of their preferred cliffs. Then they would toss a stone into the sea and jump feet first into the water to catch the stone before it disappeared into the depths. They repeated this until all the stones were gone. The Menehune who had caught the most stones was declared the winner.

At one time, in order to make a better platform for jumping, the Menehune brought a large rock from Kīpūkai. On the way, the rock broke in half. One end fell into the Hulē'ia River where it is still used as a bridge and is called **Ka-papa-o-ka-Menehune**, "causeway of the Menehune." The other half of the rock was placed at Ninini as planned.[19]

Hanamā'ulu

The upper boundary of this *ahupua'a* reaches only as far as the top of Kilohana Crater. This crater is thought to be the site of the last volcanic eruption on Kaua'i. **Kilohana**, "vantage point," implies that a fantastic view may be seen from its summit.

In the interior of the *ahupua'a* is the stream **Wai-ahi**, "fiery water," that flows from Wai-'ale'ale into the **Wai-aka**, "reflecting stream." The waters of the stream were considered a *kupua* (the body of a supernatural being). There was a village on its banks. When the August rains came and the *'o'opu* (goby fish) swarmed, the villagers prepared a bamboo fish trap and caught forty *'o'opu*. These they wrapped in *kī* leaves and broiled them over a fire. They ate every bit with relish, without a thought of sharing them with their neighbors. Later, however, they had diarrhea because the *'o'opu* were so fat. Their neighbors thought it served them right for being so greedy.[20]

Hanamā'ulu, "tired bay," was given its name because it was off the main around-the-island trail and a traveler had to walk extra miles to get there. Not only would a traveler have sore feet, but he could expect to go hungry once he reached the village.

No Hanamā'ulu ka ipu pueho.

"At Hanamā'ulu the calabash is empty."[21]

One time, some travelers from the Kona district reached the valley rim where they saw people peeling taro and heard the sound of *poi* pounders coming from the village. The travelers were pleased to know there would be fresh *poi* at the end of their journey, so they hurried down the path. When they arrived at the village, they found no *poi* at all, only villagers with sad faces apologizing for the lack of food. The visitors went hungry that night. Of course, the story was spread and from that time on the Hanamā'ulu people were known as stingy and miserly.[22]

Overlooking Hanamā'ulu Bay is **Ahu-kini,** "shrine for many blessings." Chief Ahukini lived circa 1250 A.D. and was one of the three sons of La'a-mai-kahiki, who had come from Rai'ātea in the Society Islands to visit with his foster father Mo'ikeha. Ahukini became *ali'i nui* of Puna after Ka-'ili-lau-o-ke-koa, granddaughter of Mo'ikeha, died without children of her own. On the bluff was a *heiau* of the same name. It was a medium-sized temple, but by the turn of the century only the foundations remained.

Above Hanamā'ulu is a ridge stretching to the north that begins at the peak of **Ka-lepa,** 709 feet high. The name has two meanings. The oldest meaning is "to flutter," "to wave," or "marker flag or ensign." This gives rise to the newer meaning, which is "to trade," "to sell," or "to peddle," or as a noun, "trader," "peddler," or "salesman." Anyone who had articles for barter would raise a flag to indicate that *poi* or some other article was for sale or trade.

At the foot of Kalepa there was a large *heiau,* **Ka-lau-o-ka-manu,** "tip of the endpiece of the canoe." It was greatly feared because of the many human sacrifices that were made there. The stench from the *heiau* was so bad that travelers would hurry past holding their noses. This was a large walled temple that was destroyed in 1855 to make the foundations for the Hanamā‘ulu sugar mill.

Beside it are two stones whose story remains but whose names are lost. Chief ‘U‘u-kani-pō was betrothed to Ka-lau-o-kamani, a chiefess of Hanamā‘ulu and, with a friend, Ka-ipo-lei-manu, came to see her. They were walking down the path toward Kalepa from Kilohana Crater when they were accosted by a woman. The chief recognized his betrothed, Kalauokamani. "Turn back!" she said. "Do not go near Kalauokamanu. Go toward the mountains. There you will find my sister, Moeapaki‘i. It is she you must marry." ‘U‘ukanipō realized that he was seeing the ghost of his beloved and determined to find out what had happened to her. Ignoring her warnings, the two hurried toward the village. When they came near Kalauokamanu, the stench was so strong that the two men were overcome and turned into rocks that guarded the path, warning all travelers of the danger ahead.[23]

Across the bay from Ahukini are **Nā-pali-‘o‘oma-o-Hanamā‘ulu**, "concave cliffs of Hanamā‘ulu." Here lived a young man named Pueo. It was time for him to choose a wife, but he had not found anyone on Kaua‘i who compared to the woman he saw in his dreams. He went to O‘ahu and there he heard of a young woman named Ke-‘alohi-wai. She had refused to marry any of the men her parents had presented to her, saying that the man of her dreams would come for her. When Pueo and Ke‘alohiwai met, they recognized each other immediately. They married and lived many years at Pali-‘o‘oma. After their deaths, the cliffs were renamed Ke-‘alohi-wai in honor of the dream woman from O‘ahu.[24]

To the north is **Ka-‘ili‘ili-ahi-nale**, "pebblestone of the clear fire." The name is a reference to the markers used in the game *kōnane*, a form of checkers, in which one player used white stones and the other either black or red stones. It is played on a square board and the object is to occupy as much space as possible. Perhaps there was a source of fiery red pebbles on this particular peak that a player would be delight-ed to use. This peak is the site of a story about two brothers, Wa'awa'a-iki-na'au-ao and Wa'awa'a-iki-na'au-pō. One day they went up this hill to catch chickens for their grandmother to eat. Na'auao told his brother that all the chickens with two holes in their beaks were his. Of course Na'auao got to give his grandmother chick-ens while Na'aupō had nothing. But the next time they went out, Na'aupō waited until his brother had started home with all the chick-ens. Then he covered himself with sticky gum and rolled in a heap of feathers. He ran shouting after his brother, who thought the god of birds had come to life. Na'auao dropped his chickens and ran home as fast as possible. Na'aupō gathered up the birds and presented them to his grandmother. Na'auao had outwitted himself.[25]

Wailua

The Kalepa Range, beginning in Hanamā'ulu, ends at the peak Nā-'ili-Ka'auea, "pebbles of Ka'auea." Ka'auea, a prophet from Moloka'i, came to Wailua and challenged Ka'ililauokekoa, granddaughter of Mo'ikeha, to a game of *kōnane*. She won the game and asked Ka'auea to predict her future. He told her she would become the first ruling queen of Kaua'i, but that her kingdom would not be inherited by any child of hers. The pebbles used in the game were left on this summit to honor the prophet.[26]

The ridge ends above the river at the cliff of **Mauna-kapu**, "forbid-den mountain." The god of sleep, Niolopua, lived on its slopes.

Maunakapu marked the borders of Wailuanuiho'āno. Punanuika-ia'āina, leader of the settlers from the Marquesas, placed a *kapu* on the land on either side of the river from the sea to the top of the range that divides the shore from the uplands. This area was named **Wailua-nui-a-ho'āno**, "great sacred Wailua."[27] It quickly became the seat of the royal family and center of all religious life.

Punanuikaia'āina's grandson Puna-'ai-koā-'i'i became the most famous chief of his time throughout all the Hawaiian group. His court was noted for the chivalry of his chiefs and the splendor of his feasts, which included displays of dancing. He enforced his *kapu* but was known to be merciful with those who had thoughtlessly or ignorantly broken his laws. He held the *ali'i* to strict standards, which made him popular with the commoners. Since there was no warfare during his reign, he gathered all the potential warriors around him and kept them busy in sham fights and athletic games.[28]

Puna'aikoā'i'i had only one child, the beautiful Hina-'a-ulu-ā. He had despaired of his daughter choosing a husband for herself; she had rejected every eligible male on the island. So he announced a contest: The first man to canoe from Wailua to the island of Lehua, pick up a special token that would be placed there, and return to Wailua would receive the hand of Hina'auluā. Mo'ikeha arrived on the eve of the contest. Mo'ikeha had been born on O'ahu, but had lived on Rai'ātea in the Society Islands for several years.[29] His genealogy was impeccable. Hina'auluā fell in love with him. However, Puna'aikoāi'i could not honorably cancel the contest and decided to invite Mo'ikeha to enter as a contestant. In the morning, the suitors leaped into their canoes and paddled out of sight while Mo'ikeha dawdled on the shore, talking with a more and more impatient Hina'auluā. At last Mo'ikeha entered the canoe where his *kahuna* La'amaomao was waiting, his large calabash between his knees. Their canoe easily passed through the breakers and the amazed onlookers saw Mo'ikeha hoist a sail even though the day was windless. The sail billowed as though driven by a stormy wind and the canoe zipped out of sight. In truth, La'amaomao had opened his calabash containing all the winds and, carefully modulating which winds he used, caused their canoe to sail past all others, reach Lehua for the token, and return to Wailua to claim the prize hours before any other contestant arrived.[30]

To celebrate his marriage and to consecrate the place where his

HOLOHOLOKŪ

children were to be born, Mo'ikeha ordered the building of a *heiau*, nestled at the foot of a hill about a hundred feet high, **Pu'u-kī**, *"kī* hill," on the north side of the river mouth. He named it after his priest, Holoholo-kū, (to travel here and there at will). It is the oldest known place of worship on Kaua'i that was not built by Menehune.[31]

Holoholokū became known as a *heiau* that gave special blessings from the gods to any child that was born there. A saying goes:

Hānau ke ali'i i loko o Holoholokū, he ali'i nui;

Hānau ke kanaka i loko o Holoholokū, he ali'i nō;

Hānau ke ali'i mawaho a'e o Holoholokū, 'a'ohe ali'i, he kanaka ia.

"The child of a chief born in Holoholokū is a high chief.

The child of a commoner born in Holoholokū is a chief.

The child of a chief born outside of Holoholokū is a commoner."[32]

Within the *heiau* are two boulders. The *pōhaku hānau* (birthstone) is actually two rocks. The expectant mother sat on one rock, which is flat, and rested her back on the other. When it was in use, a special house was built and these rocks would have been well covered with pandanus mats and piles of *kapa*.

After the birth, the child's umbilical cord was cut with a bamboo knife, and the cord was tied three or four inches below the cut and left intact. In about five to seven days, the cord fell off and was wrapped carefully and wedged into the *pōhaku piko* (navel rock). The fate of the navel was thought to determine what would happen to the child. If it were carelessly handled, or thrown into a refuse pit and disappeared, it was thought that the rats had eaten it and the child would grow up to be a thief, thus bringing disgrace and shame upon his parents and grandparents.[33]

When he was an old man, Mo'ikeha sent his youngest son Kila to Rai'ātea to bring back his foster son La'a, known thereafter as La'a-mai-Kahiki (La'a from foreign lands). La'a brought and stored in Holoholokū two large sharkskin drums whose deep booming was ever afterwards connected with religious ceremonies. He also introduced the coconut fiber rope and new forms of the *hula*. He brought a carved image of the god Lono-i-ka-'ou-ali'i with him. Lono was the god of agriculture, medicine, and of harvest festivities. With the image came priests who introduced new rules, rites, and customs, more rigid than the Kāne ceremonies previously followed.[34]

La'a married three O'ahu chiefesses who each bore a son on the same day. Soon afterward La'a returned to Rai'ātea. He is also the ancestor of the Cook Islanders and of the Māori of New Zealand.[35]

Ka-'ili-lau-o-ke-koa followed her grandfather Mo'ikeha as *ali'i nui*. She had inherited rank and *mana* as the senior member of her generation, and was the first female ruler of Kaua'i. She married Kaua-kahi-ali'i, who had also arrived during the migrations. He invented a nose flute to woo and win his wife.[36] After their marriage, they went surfing at **Makaīwa**, "mother of pearl eyes" (like those in a feathered image), a well-known surf near the river mouth. Ke-li'i-koa, Ka'ililauokekoa's rejected suitor and *ali'i nui* of Kona, attempted to kill Kauakahiali'i by running him down with his canoe. Kauakahiali'i survived, badly injured, but the attempt at murder had been seen by his foster mother, the powerful sorceress Waha. Alerted to the danger, Waha was able to foil several attempts on her foster son's life. These murderous attacks precipitated the first battle between the Kona and Puna kingdoms, which ended with the defeat of Kona two hundred years later.[37]

There are several possible translations of the name *Wailua*. **Wai-lua**, "two waters," derives its meaning from the two rivers that flow through the land before becoming one a mile upstream from the ocean. As **Wailua**, it could refer to "spirit of a ghost" or "spirit of one seen before or after death, separated from the body." Spirits of the dead indeed gathered together on the upland plains and on certain moonlit nights marched in great processions accompanied with drums and nose flutes down to the river. These night marchers entered waiting canoes and paddled down the river into the sea and around

MALAE

the coast until they reached Polihale at Mānā. Here they leaped
from the cliffs into Pō, the land of the dead, which lay beneath the
sea.

The Menehune, who came with Kū'alunuipaukūmokumoku, are
credited with building two *heiau* beside the banks of the Wailua.
Malae is considered the first built by them.[38] Its outside walls show a
degree of knowledge of stoneworking that was not common in Hawai'i.
They measure 273 by 324 feet and were 7 to 10 feet high and 8 feet
wide at the top. All around the inside of this wall was a ledge 6 feet
wide and 2 feet above the ground. Here people sat during the ceremonies, many of which could last a full day. Each of the four corners
of this *heiau* overlap and are buttressed with 13-foot walls, a feature
that exists in no other *heiau* in Hawai'i.[39] This *heiau* was also known
by the name **Maka-'ukiu**, "source of the *'ukiu* wind." The *'ukiu* is a
chilly northern wind not as strong as the trade winds.

POLIʻAHU

Across the river at the top of **Kuamoʻo**, "backbone," a ridge over-looking the waterfall **ʻOpae-kaʻa**, "rolling shrimp," on one side and the Wailua River on the other, lies **Poli-ʻahu** *heiau*.[40] This was a paved and walled enclosure approximately 242 feet in length and 165 feet in width, making it one of the largest *heiau* on Kauaʻi. There was a terrace on the west end with the unusual feature of a single row of stones placed on edge. This was the site of the oracle tower, a four-sided structure of wood with three floors. It was covered with white tapa and *kapu* to all but the *aliʻi nui* (ruling chief) and the *kahuna nui* (head priest). The *kahuna nui* sat alone on the top floor and, with proper prayer and ritual, waited for the advice of the gods.[41]

The two *heiau* were clearly visible to each other. Poliʻahu could communicate with Malae by means of the **Pōkahu-kani**, "bellstone," a rock that resounded with a clear loud sound when struck with a stalk of *kī*. This rock was chipped by Huleia, a Christianized priest sent by Kaʻahumanu after 1824 to destroy all vestiges of the old religion on Kaua'i.[42]

The Banks of the Wailua River

On the south shore was **Hikina-a-ka-lā**, "rising of the sun," a *pu'uhonua* (place of refuge). Warriors defeated in war and their families, as well as anyone who had broken a taboo, might flee from pursuers and enter this *heiau* where they were safe from any further pursuit. The gates were always open, but no pursuer could enter after his intended victim. The refugee would give offerings to the gods, remain within the walls for a number of days, and then be free to leave and resume his or her life. No enemy dared to touch the forgiven person, as that would have been a direct affront to the gods and retribution would swiftly follow. Inside the walls there were houses for the priests and for refugees. There was also a *pōhaku piko* (umbilical cord rock) where a leaf-wrapped afterbirth, *piko,* was placed for safekeeping. Here also those who had recovered from an illness dove into the water five times, a purification of the body after sickness.[43]

Along the shore in front of Hikinaakalā are large boulders, frequently under water, which have petroglyphs carved on them. They are said to have formed part of the wall of Hikinaakalā when the course of the river was different than it is now. These are *pōhaku ki'i* (pictured rocks). Such outstanding rocks need several stories to account for them.

A sculptor of ancient times set out to carve some idols. He finally made one that suited him and he threw all his other attempts away. These rocks are some of them, the marks being the hieroglyphics of the ancient sculptor.[44]

The demigod Māui tried to pull all the islands together with his fishhook dangling from a canoe crewed by his eight brothers. People watching from the shore commented loudly on the beautiful woman in the back of the canoe. Māui's eight brothers, although forbidden to do so, turned to look. The large fish Māui had caught broke away and the

PAEKIʻIMĀHŪOWAILUA

islands never became one landmass. Seven brothers were turned to stone and placed across the mouth of the river. The eighth was turned into a coconut tree named Niu-lolo-hiki, and from then until he was finally cut down he amused himself by dropping coconuts on the latest *aliʻi nui* whenever he passed.[45]

Kapoʻulakīnaʻu, goddess of mental health, had a bevy of young women in her company when she visited Kauaʻi and was always on the lookout for suitable husbands for them. Here at Makaīwa she saw eight young chiefs surfing. She borrowed a surfboard and joined them and one by one attempted to get one of the young men to go ashore to woo one of her maidens. The men, unfortunately for them, were more interested in each other than in the young women and refused to go ashore. Angry Kapoʻulakīnaʻu created a series of huge waves that caught the men and crushed them beneath the boiling water and

71

pushed their bodies, now turned into stone, onto the shore. These are the **Pae-ki'i-māhū-o-Wailua**, "row of homosexual images at Wailua."[46]

The brackish water of the lower Wailua River seems a strange place to find sharks. Yet ancient legends tell of at least three sharks that lived there.

The shark god Kūhaimoana, who could also take the form of a man, could often be seen working in his upriver taro patch. Whenever a group of people passed him on their way to fish, Kūhaimoana would ask them where they were going. If they were going visiting, he never replied, but if they were going fishing, he would say, "Good luck!" After they passed, he would change into his shark form, swim downriver to the sea and catch an unsuspecting victim for his meal. The people could not kill Kūhaimoana because he was a god, but they learned never to tell anyone they were going fishing. It was just too dangerous.[47]

Another shark, Kauela, used to live in a cave near the mouth of the river. The present-day cement bridge was built over it and Kauela has had to find a new home.[48]

There is a fragment of a legend that tells of two sharks, a male and a female, who lived together in the Wailua River. One day the female disappeared and from time to time the male shark would swim upriver in the hopes of finding his mate again. When disappointed, he would kill any human he found in the river on his way out to sea again.[49]

Right beside Holoholokū at the foot of Pu'ukī is another *heiau*, **Ka-lei-o-Manu**, "wreath of Manu." This *heiau* originally was about half an acre in size. In the southwest corner, there is a series of large, flat rocks piled up higher than a man's head. This was the sacrificial altar. Here pigs, chickens, fish, and dogs were sacrificed to the gods and, from time to time, humans were also sacrificed. The remains of the offerings were taken to the top of Pu'ukī and buried there. Within the *heiau* walls there was a high-peaked house that was the home of special dogs. It was the duty of the ruling priest to see that these dogs were well cared for and lacked for no comfort. It was thought that the actions of the dogs during the sacrifices gave a clue to future events.[50]

In the olden days there used to be a cave, **Ka-lua-Mōkila**, "hole of Mōkila," that ran from Puʻukī to the river. Mōkila was a *moʻo* (dragon) who had gathered all the precious stones—the diamonds, the rubies, the emeralds—of Kauaʻi into his cave. He guarded them carefully, for people tried to steal his jewels. Finally, after two men stole some gems and almost got away before being caught, Mōkila gathered up his jewels and left Kauaʻi forever, and that is why no precious stones are ever found here.[51]

In time of war, women and children belonging to the ruling family were hidden in this cave. One end of the cave was inside the *heiau* of Kaleiomanu and the other opened directly into the river. Now much of the cave has fallen in and it is very dangerous to go into it.

The plain of **Papa-ʻalae**, "plain of the mudhens" is where Māui discovered the secret of fire which, until then, had been kept by the *ʻalae* birds. The chiefess of the *ʻalae* lived in a cave at **Manu-ʻena**, "red-hot bird." Māui captured the bird by ruse and forced it to give him the secret, which consisted of rubbing two sticks together, one of soft wood and one of hard, until sparks came that could be fanned into a blaze. After he had created fire, Māui rubbed the top of the head of the *ʻalae* with a burning stick and the *ʻalae* ever since have red foreheads.[52]

About halfway up the river at a bend there is an upright, sharp-pointed rock formation, almost needlelike. Nearby there is a variegated reddish stone that seems to float in the river. Naturally there are several stories connected with them.

A chief fell in love with a common woman, but they were not permitted to marry. The gods took pity and they changed him into the rock on the side of the ridge and the woman into the rock that floats in the river.[53]

A portion of the river formed a pool called **Ka-malu**, "shade." This was the home of a *mo'o* chiefess who sometimes sat on the side of the pool as a beautiful young woman combing her long brown hair. She was the rock floating in the water. The other rock was her sister **Pōhā-kū**, "upright boulder," and had traveled as the float of an outrigger canoe from Kahiki and was borne up the Wailua river to this pool.[54]

Ka-ma'a-lau and his sister Pōhaku, warriors in the Kona army, were sent to Wailua to destroy Palila's banana grove. It was the time of war and Palila was a hero of Puna. Palila got his supernatural strength from eating bananas grown in this grove. Kama'alau and his sister slept in caves below the peak of Maunakapu. They were caught and turned to stone to guard the banana patch of Palila from thieves like themselves.

A version of this tale says that Kama'alau and his sister Pōhaku stole bananas from Palila's banana patch in the Makaleha Mountains. Discovered, they fled. Pōhaku tried to jump over the river but fell into the water where she turned to stone. Kama'alau succeeded in jumping across, but he turned back to see what had happened to his sister and he, too, was turned to stone.[55]

Palila, having helped his father overcome the Kona army and establish a truce, received a request for help from an O'ahu chief. The chief's messenger suggested that Palila disguise himself. In order to do so, Palila had himself tattooed. He stretched out on the ridge **Ka-māhū-'alele**, "homosexual messenger," at **Ka-'eli'eli-noa-a-ka-māhū**, "profound freeing of the taboo of the homosexual." One stone marks where he rested his head and another marks where his body lay during the tattooing. Palila led the O'ahu troops to victory and eventually became the *ali'i nui* of Hilo on Hawai'i.[56]

Across the river, on the north side, is **Nounou**, "to pelt," also known as the **Sleeping Giant**, for it resembles a giant stretched out on his back, his feet at the north end, a big stomach in the middle, and his face on the south.

When 'Aikanaka was the *ali'i nui* of Kaua'i, he lived in a *heiau* on

NOUNOU

top of Nounou. From here he directed the battles against his cousin Kaweloleimakua. One by one 'Aikanaka's fiercest warriors were overthrown and killed until finally Kawelo stood outside the *heiau* and called to 'Aikanaka to surrender. 'Aikanaka replied that Kawelo was only a *moa* (chicken) since he was the grandson of Chief Moa and therefore a servant of the king. This so shamed Kawelo that he almost threw himself over the cliff, but his wife pulled him back. She reminded him that the small *kāhili* whose feathers brushed 'Aikanaka's back were made of *moa* feathers and therefore a rooster was higher than a king. When 'Aikanaka heard this, he was so chagrined that he abandoned the kingdom and went to live in Wahiawa. Kawelo burned the *heiau* to signal that he had won the war and was the new ruler of Kaua'i.[57]

One legend of the Sleeping Giant says his name was Puni. While he was sleeping, a fleet of war canoes from O'ahu attacked. Puni's friends, the Menehune, tried to wake him up. They prodded him and poked him to no avail. Finally they threw huge rocks on his stomach, which bounced off and landed in the sea near the war canoes. The O'ahu fleet turned and sailed back home. The following morning the Menehune came to wake Puni up—but they could not. He was dead, for several of the rocks they had thrown during the night had fallen into his mouth as he snored and choked him to death.[58]

Another legend tells of a giant named Nunui. Wherever he stepped, he created a deep hole that the villagers planted with bananas. Nunui was very gentle and was popular with everyone. When the ruling chief wanted to gather rocks from upper Wailua and *'ōhi'a lehua* logs from the high mountains, Nunui got them all and helped build the *heiau* Kukui, which is noted for the incredibly large stones used in its walls. After a huge feast, Nunui was tired and lay down to rest. He is still sleeping there and may wake up any day.[59]

Near the junction of the two branches of the Wailua, there is a stone in the water and a large stone on the shore. Both are roughly shaped like a grass house. Both are called **Ka-hale-o-Kawelo-mahamaha-i'a**, "house of Kawelo with gills of a fish." No one entered the river here without leaving an offering of some kind. Kawelomahamahai'a was an *ali'i nui* during the seventeenth century. He had his daughter and son marry, and their child was 'Aikanaka, the first to have the rank of *nī'aupi'o* (bent coconut rib, so called because the genealogy of his mother and father both came from the same stalk). If the shadow of a *nī'aupi'o* chief fell on any object, that object became his property. If his shadow fell on a person, he or she was killed. Many people, especially children, died until all learned to watch the shadows.[60] Kawelo-mahamahai'a, it was believed, was a *kupua* (supernatural being) who could assume the forms of a man and of a shark. As a man he lived in the stone house on the shore and as a shark his home was the house in the water. He, it was whispered, would lead children to Ke'ālia where he would change into a shark and eat them all. Then he would lead Keʻālia children back to Wailua so that his shark form would have plenty to eat. Eventually the entire population between Wailua and Keʻālia lined the shore and stoned the shark to death.[61]

There is a large cave, **Māmā-akua-Lono**, "quickness of the god Lono," in a cliff overlooking the south branch of the Wailua River, just above the junction with the north branch. Long streamers of fern hang down over the opening of this cave, giving it its modern name, **Fern Grotto**. It was the home of a young woman named Māmāakualono. She had three brothers, Niolopua, Kōlea, and ʻUlili. She was skilled in the beating out of strips of mulberry bark into tapa cloth. Nearby lived a woman named Hina who wanted Māmāakualono to marry her son, but the young woman refused. Hina became very angry and dammed up the river, which slowly began to create a large reservoir. Māmāakualono did not notice this until the water began to flow into her cave. Her only escape was to jump into the water and swim to the other side. As she was swimming, Hina broke the dam and the flood of water swept the young woman out to sea. Māmāakualono called, in the form of a long chant, to her three brothers to help her. Niolopua heard his sister and he sent his two brothers, Kōlea and ʻUlili, in their bird forms to watch over her while he prayed to Lono to protect and save her. His long prayer moved the god, and he brought her ashore on Oʻahu where she crept among some *pōhuehue* (morning glory vine) and fell asleep. Two women found her there and brought her to be a wife to their brother Moku-ʻula. Māmāakualono began to beat out tapa until her new house was filled with thousands of articles of clothing and bedding, real wealth in ancient times. Then she left and returned to Wailua and her cave, where she lived until she died. Lono turned the three brothers into rocks where they could keep watch over their sister as she lived in her cave and make sure Hina never dammed up the river again.[62]

Manamana-i-aka-luea, "branches that cause a reflection that

WAIʻEHU

makes one seasick," was an *'ōhi'a lehua* tree that grew on the bank of the river below Māmāakualono's cave. No blossoms were ever seen on the tree, but the tree's reflection within the river showed it in full bloom. At certain times of the year, the flowers would bob to the surface, float down the river and out into the ocean where they eddied in a great circle at **Lehua-wehe**, "open *'ōhi'a lehua* blossoms," in front of Hauola.

'A'ā-hoaka, "brilliant light of Hoaka," is a rounded cinder cone 802 feet high between the two branches of the Wailua River. This hill was named after a young chief who lived here. He was particularly handsome, and it was said that he shone and flashed and his brightness was like lightning or the brightness of the second night of the moon.[63]

There is a large waterfall in the south branch of the Wailua River. Today it is called **Wailua Falls**, but its ancient name is **Wai-'ehu**, "spraying water." Kaumuali'i, last king of Kaua'i, jumped over these falls into the pool below for sport. Nowadays this is extremely dangerous because over half the former water flow has been diverted for sugarcane irrigation.

Behind Wai'ehu there was a cave called **Ke-ana-o-Kawelo-wai**, "cave of Kawelo-wai." It has now fallen in, but in olden days Wailua chiefesses hid here in time of war. To enter the cave, one had to dive under the falls with a weighted rope tied about one's waist. The other end was held by a friend to keep the swimmer from being swept downstream and drowned in the force of the water. Then one crawled into a long cave that was very windy.

Just above the falls there was a row of large rocks across the stream used as stepping-stones. Before there were rocks, Wailua, a *mo'o*, lived beside the river. She owned a long wooden plank that she would stretch across from one bank to another if she were paid a toll by the traveler. If she felt cheated, she would shake the plank when the traveler reached the middle and dump him over the falls. Pele's sister, Hi'iaka, came to this crossing on her way to Hā'ena. She asked Wailua to throw the plank across and the *mo'o* refused at first but finally did as asked. Then as soon as Hi'iaka had reached the halfway point, the *mo'o* tried to turn the plank over. Hi'iaka regained the shore safely and killed the *mo'o*. Then she threw large rocks across the river so she could step safely across.[64]

In 1824, after the disastrous rebellion of George Humehume, Queen Regent Ka'ahumanu came to Kaua'i to see for herself this island she had conquered. While she was resting at Wailua, Pāmāhoa wandered into the presence of the Dowager Queen. Pāmāhoa had lost her husband during the rebellion and carried his bones wrapped up in a bundle. Ka'ahumanu was outraged and ordered the woman killed. Two Kaua'i guards led Pāmāhoa up the river but then told her to run away for they had no desire to kill her. She did, and came at last to Wai'ehu. As she began to cross the stream, a sudden spate of water and a gust of wind struck her, tearing the bundle of bones out of her arms. Pāmāhoa leaped over the falls to join her husband. Sometimes her cry as she fell can still be heard echoing from the cliffs.[65]

Pu'u-pilo, "hill of the swampy odor," is a hill on the north bank. Prisoners were herded up the hill and driven off the south wall, which slopes directly down to the river bottom.

Pihana-ka-lani, "gathering place of high supernatural beings," was a *heiau* built by the sorceress Waha to house herself and her two foster children. The boy was Kauakahiali'i, who invented the nose flute and with its plaintive, five-note melody lured the princess of Puna, Ka'ililauokekoa, to him. Waha's daughter was Ka-hale-lehua, who became the goddess of rain and who also had a home on the floor of the channel between O'ahu and Kaua'i. Even when it was new, Pihanakalani was difficult to find, for Waha hid the paths leading to it. Today its location is unknown.[66]

For a period of almost two hundred years, approximately between 1150 and 1350 A.D., there were many wars between the Kona and Puna chiefdoms. During this time, Ke-āhua was a chief of Wailua.

Keāhua and his wife Kauhao had a son named Ka-uʻi-lani. His father's parents bathed him as an infant in the spring **Wai-uʻi**, "youthful water," which gave him great strength and beauty. The family lived contentedly at Wailua, but one day the chief of Kona sent a dragon to destroy Puna. This *moʻo* was Akua-pehu-lani, who could take the form of a man or a seagoing dragon. He easily defeated the Puna forces. Keāhua and his family retreated to a valley far up the Wailua River. There they lived until Kauʻilani grew up. His father's parents gave him a *malo* named Pā'ihi-kū, which gave the young man's spear the strength to penetrate anything it was thrown at. Kauʻilani conceived a method to defeat the dreadful dragon. He ordered a thick row of bamboo to be planted across the lower part of the valley and had a row of carved images set up behind that. When all was ready, Kauʻilani prayed to his gods and they entered the row of images, bringing them to life. He ordered the bamboo cut down, leaving each stump with a sharp-pointed end. Then he went down to the sea and insulted the dragon until it was so outraged that it chased the young man back into the mountains. The dragon was charging so fast that it did not see the bamboo and impaled itself. The gods speared and clubbed the *moʻo* with their war clubs. Then Kauʻilani threw his spear and it went clean through Akuapehulani, ending his life and his oppression. The valley is named after **Ke-āhua**, "hillock."[67]

Olohena

Olohena is a narrow *ahupuaʻa* sandwiched between Waipouli and Wailua. The use of its name has all but disappeared as it calls to mind two hills whose shape resembles a pair of buttocks.

After Kawelo defeated ʻAikanaka, he built a *heiau* in Olohena that he named **Ka-iki-hāuna-kā**, "little striking blow." It was built as a place to make an offering to his war god of the first enemy warrior to have been killed in battle. This would have been one of the warriors Kawelo killed as his canoe was carried onto shore. Until that moment ʻAikanaka had not been sure Kawelo was aboard. Kawelo was given time to set up his camp and feed his men before the first formal battle began.[68]

Nearby there once was a special house built for ho'opāpā, the art of riddling. It was surrounded by a fence made of the bones of those who had lost the game. Its name was **Hale-pā-iwi**, "house enclosed with bones." Halepākī came from Hawai'i to challenge chief Ka-lani-ali'i-loa and his experts, but he lost and his bones were added to the fence. Halepākī's son, Kai-palaoa, came to challenge his father's killers. In a long duel of words, Kaipalaoa overcame his opponents and was able to take his father's bones home for a proper burial.[69]

Kukui, "candlenut tree" or "enlightenment," was a huge walled *heiau* located on the headland of **Lae-'ala-kukui**, "point of the scent of *kukui*." This *heiau* is built of extremely large stones, some of them weighing several tons. The giant Nunui collected the stones and put them in position and gathered the *'ōhi'a lehua* logs from the mountains to build all the structures within the walls. After it was built, he was tired and stretched out on the nearby hilltop, where he still sleeps.[70]

Waipouli

Wai-pouli, "dark water," is the *ahupua'a* south of Kapa'a and north of Olohena. It is possible that an eclipse of the sun was observed here that gave it this name.

On the seacoast, the boundary point between Waipouli and Kapa'a is **Ka-lua-pā-lepo**, "pit for dirty dishes." The boundary with Olohena was at **Kaunana-wa'a**, "mooring place for canoes." There were six house clusters, called villages in the Māhele records, whose names give an insight into the ancient society: **Kāne-limua**, "man overgrown with moss"; **Maka-lokoloko**, "eyes swelling up in tears"; **Makamaka-'ole**, "without an intimate friend"; **Mokuna-hele**, "traveling district"; **Nā-hale-ka-wawā**, "houses where there is lots of noise."

Hi'iaka and Lohi'au were reunited at Waipouli. Hi'iaka had been sent by her sister Pele, the volcano goddess, to bring Lohi'au, a chief of Hāʻena, to her on Hawaiʻi. After many adventures, Hiʻiaka returned to Pele with Lohiʻau, but she found that Pele had broken her promise to protect Hiʻiaka's grove of *lehua* trees. Heartbroken, Hiʻiaka kissed Lohiʻau for the first time, for she had fallen in love with him during the voyage. Pele covered Lohiʻau with lava and Hiʻiaka returned to Kauaʻi, vowing never to see her sister again. Two of Pele's brothers took pity on Lohiʻau and brought him back to life. When he arrived at Hanamāʻulu, he found two old men preparing sheets of *kapa* to take to Waipouli as gifts to honor the marriage of Hiʻiaka and Paoa. Paoa had sworn to avenge his friend Lohiʻau but became Pele's lover instead. Lohiʻau asked the old men to help him get to Waipouli without being seen. They folded their *kapa* sheets over a carrying pole, and when the pole stretched from one man's shoulder to the other, Lohiʻau hid beneath the fold. When they reached Waipouli, the old men joined in a game of *kilu*, a favorite pastime. Hiʻiaka tossed her *kilu*, a coconut marker, and hit the marker of one of the old men. Sadly she chanted a song that she and Lohiʻau had created on their travels together. A voice joined her, somehow knowing the correct words. Hiʻiaka looked around but saw no one and thinking she was perhaps imagining things, she continued the game, this time hitting the marker of the other old man. Once again she chanted and the unknown voice joined in. Hiʻiaka knew that this chant had been created on the volcano's edge as the lava approached them and she knew no one else would know the words. She rushed to the *kapa* and brushed it aside to find Lohiʻau. Hiʻiaka and Lohiʻau were married and lived the rest of their lives at Hāʻena.[71]

Mākaha-o-Kūpānihi, "Kūpānihi is fierce" or "star of Kūpānihi," was a deep pool set aside for the *aliʻi* to bathe in. Mākaha is a star near the Pleiades. It and another star named Mākohi-lani were patrons of fighters. Kūpānihi was the god invoked by the experts when carving out a canoe. This is where Keawe, the half-brother of Kaumualiʻi, was shot. When their mother died on the battlefield with her husband

Kā'eo-Kū-lani, Kaumuali'i was only twelve years old and the heir apparent. Keawe, in his mid-twenties, seized his younger brother and all the guns and ammunition on the island and declared himself *ali'i nui*. Keawe's father was a Kaua'i chief, whereas Kā'eo had come from Maui. Keawe did not altogether trust the Maui chiefs who had come with his stepfather, but did accept the companionship of Ki'ikikī and his brother. They, realizing that their ambition to become overlords of the districts would not be fulfilled, suggested that Keawe take a tour around the island. Keawe did, and when they reached Waipouli, Keawe went to bathe in this pool. The two Maui chiefs, hoping to win the favor of Kaumuali'i by their action, shot Keawe and took the guns and ammunition. They then thought Kaumuali'i would reward them as they hoped. Instead Kaumuali'i had them killed.[72]

Kapa'a

Ka-pa'a, "solid," is one of the largest *ahupua'a* of the Puna District and the most bereft of legends. It was famous for its *kalukalu*, a reed that grew in the marshes that stretched along the entire shoreline just behind the sand dunes. The *kalukalu* was woven into mats that were stronger and more durable than pandanus mats. A *kalukalu* mat was laid on the ground under a tree, covered with a thick pile of grass, and a second mat was thrown over that for a comfortable outdoor bed. There were no mosquitoes in the ancient days. Lovers enjoyed whiling away the time in the *kalukalu* grass, for it was soft enough to be comfortable and tall enough for secrecy.

The pond of **Kolokolo**, "soap plant," was also popular, for the fresh water was deep and it was lined with *kolokolo*, whose leaves form a lather in water. This plant was used as soap throughout Polynesia and certainly was one of the plants the earliest settlers brought with them.

The headland on the north is **Ke-ahiahi**, "twilight." Here lived a boy, Pāka'a, with his mother and uncle. He knew nothing of his father, and the fishermen would tease him about that whenever he went down to the beach where they were preparing to canoe beyond the reef to catch *mālolo* (flying fish), which was his favorite food. He always asked to go and was always refused. He would sit on the brow of the headland and stare at the canoes as they paddled out to the deep-sea fishing grounds. He studied the waves and the winds and wondered how he could get all the *mālolo* he and his family could eat. As sometimes happens, an idea blossomed in full detail. Pāka'a wove a sail that looked like a crab claw and attached it to his uncle's canoe. Test runs showed that this sail, filled with wind, drove his small, lightweight canoe through the water with incredible speed. The next time the fishermen went out, Pāka'a paddled after them. Being only one boy, his canoe moved very slowly compared to an eight-man canoe. Once at the deep-sea grounds, Pāka'a caught a few fish of his own. At the end of the day, Pāka'a challenged the fishermen, betting he could beat them to shore. The fishermen laughed but, taunted by Pāka'a, finally accepted the bet. Pāka'a insisted that his canoe be filled with fish, saying that he was too little against such big men and that if they lost there was no way he could force them to keep their promise, but if he lost, they would have no trouble collecting the fish from him.

The fishermen began paddling toward shore. They watched as Pāka'a paddled farther out to sea and began to fumble with a pole that had a mat tied to it. It looked so funny that they began to laugh, and soon they lost the rhythm of their own paddling. Suddenly Pāka'a's mast was up and the sail filled with wind. Pāka'a turned toward shore and shot past the astonished fishermen, landing on the beach far ahead of them. That night, Pāka'a, his mother, and his uncle had all the *mālolo* they could eat.[73]

Keālia

Ke-ālia lies between Kamalomalo'o and Kapa'a and stretches along its river to a peak that overlooks Hanalei Valley. The name means "salt encrustation," "salt land," or "salt pan," all three translations indicat-

85

ing that this was a source of salt, so necessary for preserving fish and for flavoring *poi*.

When Hi'iaka and Wahine-'ōma'o, on their journey to Hā'ena, arrived at Keālia, they came upon a man cooking *lū'au* (young taro leaves) to eat with his *poi*. Hi'iaka by her magic power cooked the *lū'au* in a few minutes. Looking into the man's house, Hi'iaka saw a very sick woman. The man told her that none of the *kahuna* he had called on had been able to help her. Hi'iaka uttered a prayer and at once health was given back to the woman.[74]

Wai-pahe'e, "slippery water," is a slanted waterfall. The stream has carved a rounded channel that is moss covered. The slide falls into a deep pond. A swimmer can sit at the top, blocking the channel until a body of water is built up; then, pushing off, he or she has an exhilarating slide into the pool below.

Kaweloleimakua and Kauahoa, as youngsters, accompanied 'Aikanaka here on an excursion. The two boys had a contest as to which could weave a better *lei* for their chief. Kauahoa made one of *liko lehua* buds of the *lehua* tree, and Kawelo tried to make one of fern. His fell apart almost as fast as he could make it. Kauahoa was declared winner. Kawelo immediately challenged the other to a *na'ina'i mimi* (a urination contest) to see which one could urinate the longest. Since Kawelo was small and Kauahoa became famed as the last gigantic hero and was already far bigger than Kawelo, he lost this contest, too, and wondered if he was always fated to lose any contest with his birthmate. When at last the two met on a battlefield, Kawelo fondly recalled this excursion to Kauahoa in the hopes that the memory of the days they had spent together as children would end the present conflict between them. Unfortunately it did not and Kauahoa was killed.[75]

Kamalomalo'o

The northernmost *ahupua'a* of Puna is **Ka-malo-malo'o**, "dry loincloth." In olden days, when an *ali'i* came ashore from a canoe voyage or surfing, his bodyguards threw their spears at him. It was a mark of chiefly strength that he could dodge or catch every spear. After this, he was ceremoniously given a dry *malo* (a piece of tapa about a foot and a half wide by several yards long, the principal clothing for men).[76]

Āhihi, "plant with long runners and creepers," is a headland that lies halfway along the oceanfront. The plain behind it is 'A'aka, "grumbling," and the valley beside it is Hō-mai-ka-wa'a, "bring me the canoe," all three names connected to the same story. 'A'aka, a Menehune, loved to jump into the ocean after a stone, but he always found something to grumble about. Once when they were jumping from Āhihi Point, 'A'aka leaped in, almost into the mouth of a large white shark, but he managed to scramble ashore in one piece. Angrily he stared at the shark who was ruining his sport. Then he saw how he could catch this shark, which was so big it could swallow a Menehune whole. 'A'aka told his companions to weave a huge net of the *āhihi* vines that grew around them, and when it was through, he ordered, *"Hō mai ka wa'a!"* "Bring the canoe!" It was not his place to give orders as he was not the chief of the party, but nonetheless the canoe was brought, the net put in, and the Menehune put to sea to do battle. They managed to catch the shark and tow it onto the reef at 'Aliomanu.[77]

Māhu-nā-pu'u-one, "vapor that rises from the sand dunes," was a *heiau* where humans were sacrificed. It was built in the late 1600s by Kawelomahamahai'a to celebrate the birth of his twin grandsons who were owners of the dreaded *kapu moe* (prostration taboo). Everyone had to lie flat on the ground in the presence of these two boys. Failure to do so was death. The only people exempt from this *kapu* were Kaweloleimakua and Kauahoa, who had been born on the same day in the same place as the twins. They were allowed to sit in 'Aikanaka's presence. This new and fearful rank was given to children whose parents were brother and sister. The birth of these twins marked the beginning of interisland warfare that ended in the destruction of a great number of the *ali'i* of Hawai'i and in the collapse of the religious system itself.[78]

Like the kingdom of Puna, the *heiau* no longer exists.

Ko'olau District

*T*he district of Ko'olau, on the northeast side of the island, occupies a narrow strip between the sea and the ridge named **Maka-leha**, "eyes that glance upward." Part of the area is dry, yet all of Ko'olau receives adequate rainfall for dryland farming. Small streams, mainly fed by springs, offered only enough water for a limited number of taro fields. The shore is lined by many bays and reefs, which provided rich sources of food. The district's name, **Ko'olau**, "windward," occurs on many other Polynesian islands and designates the side of the island that faces the trade winds.

Ko'olau was divided into ten *ahupua'a*, some reaching the top of Makaleha. These land divisions are unusual in that, except for Anahola, they are all very small—smaller than some of the *'ili* in other districts.

An ancient saying perhaps offers an explanation:

Hao ka Ko'olau, pau nā mea aloha,

Ahu iho ka ua wahawaha i Wailua.

"Ko'olau was robbed of all endeared things,

The despised blossoms were collected together at Wailua."[1]

It was formerly the practice of chiefs to punish lawbreakers for all offenses that did not carry the death penalty by stripping them entirely of their property. Did a chief of Ko'olau rebel against his ruling chief and lose? The legends are silent.

Anahola

Anahola contains 6,327 acres and is the largest of Ko'olau's *ahupua'a*. Anahola's shoreline stretches from **Papa-loa**, "long reef," on the east to **Kuaehu**, "lonely," on the west. The upper portion of the valley had taro terraces, but only the flatlands along the river mouth were heavily cultivated. Anahola is named after a *mo'o*, a lizard *kupua* that appeared on land as a man and in the sea as a merman.[2]

Within the river was the pond **Alaweo**, named for a native shrub of the goosefoot family that grew on the banks of the pond. Young plants, leaves, and plant tips were eaten, usually wrapped in *kī* leaves and cooked on hot coals. The *mo'o* Pehu-iki was the guardian of the pond. He had three daughters who were often seen sitting on the banks of the Alaweo combing their long hair. At night the four *mo'o* slept in the cave of Hāhā-lina, "to grope through the stickiness."

The *ahupua'a* is dominated by the peak Hōkū-'alele, "star-messenger," "shooting star," or "comet," the first peak on the ridge. There was a three-terraced, paved temple about a hundred feet square with a low wall on top of this peak. From the prayer tower, the prophet Hulu-māniani saw a rainbow shining over the pool on O'ahu where the young woman Lā'ie-i-ka-wai had been hidden by her guardian-grand-mother Waka. Lā'ieikawai's father had sworn he would kill all his daughters that were born before he had a son, and so Lā'ieikawai and her twin sister were separated at birth and hidden for their safety. Hulumāniani went to O'ahu, but Waka, upset at being discovered, moved her ward to Hawai'i. Hulumāniani announced that Lā'ieikawai would eventually settle on Kaua'i and he would await her arrival. After many adventures, Lā'ieikawai went to live with Hulumāniani in Hanakoa Valley before settling in Wailua. After she was betrayed by her husband and her twin sister, her parents built a village in Mānā for her and she became known as *ka wahine o ka li'ulā,* "the woman of the mirage."[3]

There is a large rectangular rock on the slopes of Hōkū'alele that was once a man who was punished by being turned to stone. Lahema-nu was the beautiful daughter of an Anahola chief. She was so lovely and desirable that, when she went to bathe each day in the clear pool beneath the cliff, her father always sent a companion maid with her to keep close watch while she was in the water. The lithe, nymphlike body of the girl cutting the surface of the clear water was a form for the gods to envy. One day the maid told Lahemanu that she was sure a strange man had preceded them to the pool and had hidden in the bushes where he might feast his eyes on her. Frightened and furious, but determined to have her daily bath, Lahemanu sought the aid of a powerful *kahuna*. The next day on their trip to the pool, he accompanied them. Lahemanu directed the *kahuna* to watch carefully and if he caught sight of the man to punish him at once. The *kahuna* nodded and while Lahemanu bathed, he gazed intently at the surrounding bushes. Suddenly he spotted gleaming eyes peering out through the leaves. Upon discovery, the unknown man took to his heels and fled. When he got halfway up the mountain, he had to rest. Then it was that the *kahuna* exerted his mystic powers and turned him to stone.[4]

'Aliomanu

The *ahupua'a* of 'Ali-o-manu, "scar made by birds," is very small but has a fringing reef, sandy beach, and excellent *kula* land rising to the foot of the mountains where the land abruptly climbs to the high peak of **Kalalea**, "prominent,"[5] which is beside Hōkū'alele. This peak resembles the fin of a shark or porpoise as it cleaves the surface of the sea. The word *kalalea* is used in chants to figuratively imply that one is haughty. The peak, it is said, was once a warrior who responded snobbishly to a woman who loved him. He was turned into this peak and she into the neighboring peak, which still seems to lean yearningly toward him.[6]

Pu'u-ana-kō-ua, "hill of the cave towed in the rain," the "Hole in the Mountain" of former times, was such a visible and distinct feature that naturally many stories arose to account for it.

Kaweloleimakua and Kauahoa, giant hero of Hanalei, fought each other in Wailua. Kawelo threw his spear, but Kauahoa ducked. The spear flew on—after casting its shade on the coconut trees at Niumalu—and pierced the mountain, creating the hole.[7]

A chief of Anahola had a beautiful daughter and rich fields of *'awa*. A huge *kupua* rat came at night and destroyed the chief's *'awa* fields as well as feasting on the farmer's crops. Along the foot of the mountain it had worn a trail through the grasslands from Moloa'a where it

KALALEA AME PUʻUANAKŌUA

made its home. It became known as **Ke-ala-a-ka-ʻiole**, "trail made by the rat." Furious, the chief offered his daughter in marriage to whoever would kill the rat. There were many competitors, but the reward went to a Prince Kawelo from Oʻahu. He hid on the inland side of Makaleha and when he heard the rat passing on the other side, he threw his spear. It pierced the ridge, knocking out a huge rock that fell and killed the rat. The hole in the mountain shows where the rock was dislodged by the spear.[8]

Unfortunately, not long ago the roof of the hole collapsed, and today only the merest hint in the shape of the crescent moon can still be seen.

The story behind the *ahupuaʻa*'s name begins at Hōmaikawaʻa in

Kamalomalo‘o. There ‘A‘aka, a Menehune, caught a shark by weaving a fish trap of *huehue,* a native climber that grew at ‘Ahihi Point. After a fearsome ride, the weakened shark was brought to shore at the reef here. ‘A‘aka wanted the sharkskin as a souvenir, but sea birds, attracted by the bonanza, flocked to the carcass and began to devour it. ‘A‘aka tried to chase them off but was attacked by them instead, leaving him with the souvenir of a scar on his face.[9]

Pāpa‘a

Pā-pa‘a, "secure enclosure," is also small. It has a reef, bay, and *kula* land as well as a small mountain valley named **Kihe**, a small native fern *(Xiphopteris saffordii).* A cinder cone 329 feet high marks the boundary with Moloa‘a on the west. Its name is **Pūweuweu**, "clump of greenery" (especially a bouquet of greens placed on the altar to honor Laka, goddess of the hula). It is also the name of a chanted prayer to Laka designed to free the *kapu* from a *hula* student at the end of a period of training.[10]

There was a *heiau* located on the hilltop that was a place of refuge. A wrongdoer, or someone escaping the perils of war, could take shelter here and, after a series of prayers and ceremonies were done, was free to leave and pick up his or her life unmolested.

The *heiau* that gives the *ahupua‘a* its name was located at **Ka-wai-papa**, "flat water." This was a walled *heiau* sixty by eighty feet in size. The walls were five feet wide and about four feet high. The *heiau* was dedicated to Ka-hō-ali‘i, a god sometimes associated with the underworld.[11]

Kahōali‘i was the possessor of two famous axes: Hau-mapu, "swooping breeze," and ‘Olopū, "blistered." The *kahuna* who selected the *‘ōhi‘a lehua* tree for the building of a *heiau* for human sacrifice had to touch the tree with Haumapu and ‘Olopū before it could be felled and brought down from the forest.

On various ceremonial occasions, Kahōali‘i was impersonated as a dark man, completely naked, with stripes or patches of white on the inner sides of his thighs. At the *makahiki* festival, which occurred every winter, the eyeball of a fish and that of a human victim were given him to swallow. At the building of a human sacrifice *heiau*, the god was again impersonated by a naked man. At the dedication ceremony of a *heiau* for the circumcision of a young chief, a night was given to Kahōaliʻi during which anyone who came outside his or her house was killed. The priests who sought human sacrifices were skilled at enticing the unwary out of their homes in order to secure a victim.[12] After the coming of the Pele family, Kahōaliʻi became confused with Pele's brother Kamoho-aliʻi, the shark god.

Moloaʻa

The hills of **Molo-aʻa**, "tangled roots," used to be thickly overgrown with *wauke*, the paper mulberry used for *kapa*. Thus it was said that the *aʻa* (roots) of the wauke were *molo* (matted) together.[13]

Moloaʻa is a classic valley *ahupuaʻa*, sloping gently from the mountains, ever widening as it nears the sea. Its bay is the second largest of Koʻolau. It had a good stream that watered many terraces along its three-mile course toward the sea. A half mile of relatively flat land inland from its bay was all terraced beautifully. Near the shore the soil consists of sand mixed with humus, which makes it ideal for sweet potatoes.

Moloaʻa is still famous for the quality of its edible *limu* (seaweed). The *limu kohu* was brought here from South Kohala, on the island of Hawaiʻi by a chief of that place. The *limu* was placed under *kapu* and strictly reserved for the use of the *aliʻi nui*. A beach and land section on the plains to the west of the valley is **Kaʻakaʻa-niu**, "rolling of the coconut," where the quality of seaweed was considered the finest on the island.

At the foot of **Ka-lae-o-ulu-ʻoma**, "cape of the baked breadfruit," a headland on the eastern side of the bay, there is a spring of fresh water

95

in the reef. Only those who know where it is can find the pure sweet water of **Ka-wai-a-Maliu,** "spring dug by Maliu." Maliu was a Menehune who had asthma and so did not enjoy the sport of leaping feet first into the ocean after a pebble to catch it before it disappeared in the ocean depths. While his friends played, Maliu wandered the countryside and met a young Hawaiian woman. They fell in love and had a child. It was many months before Maliu was missed, but one day his chief realized he had not seen Maliu for some time. The chief sent all the other Menehune to find Maliu, but with the aid of his wife, Maliu got to the beach undetected and onto the reef where he began digging in a sand-filled hole. Curious, the chief asked what he was doing. "Digging for fresh water," Maliu said. "If there is fresh water, you will live," said the chief. "If not, you will die." Maliu kept digging and soon a gush of fresh, sweet water flowed up. Maliu was saved.[14]

Lepeuli

Lepe-uli, "dark cockscomb," is very small and does not reach the mountains. There are no surviving legends attached to this *ahupua'a,* and only two of its place-names offer clues to ancient life.

Ka-'ume-ka-'iwa, "allure of the man-of-war bird," was a houselot with six *lo'i* (wet taro fields) at the beach. It was named after the *'iwa,* the frigate or man-of-war bird, which is a seagoing bird whose wingspan can reach seven feet from tip to tip, although it is rare to see one so large. It feeds by forcing other, smaller fishing birds to vomit their catch, which the *'iwa* scoops up in midair. Whenever the *'iwa* flies over shore, it is a sign of impending bad weather. Because of its method of feeding, the *'iwa* was used figuratively to mean a thief. Because it is conspicuous, it also figuratively meant a handsome person of either sex, someone who stood out from the crowd because of his or her good looks.

Ka-lama-'ula, "red lama wood," was formerly a pasture area. *Lama* refers to all endemic kinds of ebony. The framework of certain special huts was built of its wood. These huts were built in one period of day-light *(lama)* and the sick were placed inside the hut for curing. A block of *lama* was also placed on *hula* altars because its name suggested enlightenment, since the word also means a torch, light, or lamp.

Waipakē

Wai-pakē, "brittle water," approximately 706 acres in size, has an excellent reef and extensive upland country suitable for dry land farming. It is cut off from the mountains by Lepeuli *ahupuaʻa*, which lies both on the south and east sides. Pīlaʻa lies on the west. Taro was grown wherever the land could be irrigated. There was no steadily flowing stream, but a series of springs supplied the necessary water.

Noni, a plant grown for dye and medicine, grew in the uplands, as well as the edible and bitter gourds. The small gourds were used as food and water receptacles, while bitter gourds provided calabashes large enough for clothing and net storage.

The story behind the naming of this *ahupuaʻa* concerns two women pounding *poi*. The *poi* of the first one made a popping sound—*pakē*—whenever it was mixed or stirred. The second woman teased the first and sat down to pound some *poi*. But her *poi* too was *pakē*, and the *ahupuaʻa* was named Wai-pakē after these two.[15]

Ke-puhi, "blowhole," a small cave on the table rock, is the north-western boundary point between Pīlaʻa and Waipakē. The sea has access to it through an arch, forming a blowhole where the ocean enters a lava tube and spews up in a fountain.

Pīlaʻa

Pīlaʻa, containing 1,250 acres, is fronted by a reef and a sandy beach reaching from Kepuhi to Pōhaku-malumalu, "sheltering stone," on the border with Waiakalua. There is a narrow plain between the beach and a low cliff that is broken by two gulches, one carved by the Pīlaʻa Stream, the other by the Kānoa. Above the low *pali* there is a gently

PŌHAKUMALUMALU

KAUKAHE

rising plain dominated by a cinder cone 761 feet high. The plain rises to a ridge 800 feet above sea level that marks the end of the *ahupuaʻa*, far short of the mountains.

This must have posed a problem in paying taxes during the annual *makahiki* season, for one of the tributes demanded each year was a supply of feathers from colorful mountain birds. The solution may be indicated by the name of a cultivated field, **Ka-moa-ʻahuʻula**, "feather cloak (made out of) chicken (feathers)."

Kānoa, "ʻ*awa* bowl," Valley was named after a large stone that had been carved to form a bowl in the top in which ʻ*awa* was placed. When the bowl was filled, the liquid drained down a groove into waiting coconut cups.

At the top of Kānoa Valley was **Kau-kahe**, "flowing chants," the largest and oldest grove of *kukui* trees on Kauaʻi. The trunks were of immense size, and at one place the branches met overhead to form an open space that early Western visitors described as cathedral-like. This glade was called **Kau-hau-keke'e,** "hang of the crooked *hau* tree." Within this grove was **Hā-'ula-o-Lono,** "red stem of Lono," a walled *heiau* about forty feet square. It was well paved inside with water-smoothed pebbles.

From time to time, the high chiefs and high priests of Kaua'i would gather within the grove of Kaukahe and the *heiau* was rededicated, Lono given his proper sacrifices, and official business was conducted. Afterward there was a feast and entertainment and the drinking of *'awa.*

On one such occasion, the *konohiki* (headman) of Pīla'a gave a feast so memorable it has not been forgotten. First he ordered bundles of cooked fish brought from all the mountain streams especially famed for having the best-tasting *'o'opu* on the island. He ordered Kānoa to be filled with *'awa* made from fresh roots brought from **Ka-lua-'ā,** "rocky pit," a narrow valley of the Waimea Canyon complex. *'Awa* from Kalua'ā was particularly potent.

Meanwhile, his wife was also busy. She brought anise-scented berries of *mokihana* from the cliffs of **Ka-hili-kolo,** "creeping tangle," and dark-backed shrimp from the stream of **Ka-lua-o-ka-lani,** "pit of heaven."

The high chief was delighted with his entertainment and before he left, he named the nearby grassy hill after the *konohiki* chief, **Ka-moku.** He gave the wife an *ahupua'a* of her own, making sure that the bottomlands of the Kīlauea River from waterfall to mouth were included. This was given her name: **Kāhili,** "feather standard."[16]

Waiakalua

Wai-a-ka-lua, "water of the pit," was divided into two areas: **Waia-kalua-iki** and **Waiakalua-nui.** The streams of this *ahupua'a* are all fed from springs. There were taro fields in the valleys. The houselots were between the fields and on the ridge between the two streams.

A boy was born in Waiakalua in about 1790 and was trained to be a warrior. He was an expert at spear dodging, slinging, bone breaking, and other martial skills. He became one of Kaumualiʻi's guards and was tattooed on one leg from hip to foot. This tattooing of the king's immediate guard was a reminder that Kaumualiʻi's uncle, King Kahekili of Maui, was similarly tattooed. This young man must have been very tall, as one of the requirements for his position was to be seven feet in height.

After Kaumualiʻi died in 1824, a battle was waged between Humehume, Kaumualiʻi's oldest son, and the forces of Kamehameha II. The Kauaʻi warriors attacked Fort Hipo at Waimea and were repulsed. They retreated to the plains of Hanapēpē and Wahiawa, armed with traditional wooden weapons. The Kamehameha forces, armed with Western weapons, defeated the Kauaʻi forces easily.

For two weeks after this battle, the Kamehameha forces hunted the defeated in order to destroy them—man, woman, and child—once and for all. All men with "black legs" were killed on sight. When the Kamehameha forces arrived at Waiakalua they found the young man hiding in a woman's sacred house. He was led out before a firing squad. The young warrior refused to have his hands bound and stood facing the soldiers. As the command "Fire!" was given, the young warrior ducked, ran forward at top speed, grabbed two of the rifles from the soldiers, and pushing past them, escaped.

From then on, this young warrior had the name Nā-pū-ʻelua, "two rifles." After an amnesty was declared, Nāpūʻelua returned to Waiakalua, where he lived peacefully. In the Māhele of 1848, he laid claim to some land, which he received two years later. He is the last known "black leg," the last of the honor guard that protected the person of the king.[17]

Kāhili

Kāhili, "feather standard," is dominated by the 2,060-foot peak of **Ka-lau-pala**, "fern frond."

The *kāhili* was the mark of royalty and was carried by those in attendance to the high chief or chiefess. Feathers were tied together in small bundles, then attached to a highly polished stick of some precious wood. The wood and pattern of feathers indicated the rank of the *aliʻi*.

The *ahupuaʻa* is named after a chiefess who, with her husband, catered a memorable feast to the guests assembled in the *kukui* forest of Kauhale in Pīlaʻa.

Wai-a-ʻula, "water becoming red," is a pond near the mouth of Kāhili Stream. Waiaʻula was a *lua-moʻo* (a dragon hole) belonging to Kihawahine, a dreaded man-killing goddess. The place was taboo to all except the chiefs who went there to swim. At certain times, the water gushed up in the spring so that part of the water was red and part remained dark as before. When the water became red, it was a sign of the return of Kihawahine, who, like other *moʻo,* could transform her body into different colors and shapes. The red water was the body of Kihawahine.[18]

Kīlauea

The streams of **Kī-lau-ea,** "spewing of many vapors," that flow between the Makaleha Mountains and the ridge named **Ka-moʻo-koa,** "brave lizard," have formed deep gulches. Although this meant the arable land was too high above the stream to be irrigated for wetland farming, there are, nonetheless, the remains of three long irrigation ditches so ancient that legend says they are the claw marks of a *moʻo.* This lizard had been ordered by Mano-ka-lani-pō to open Kīlauea's upper regions for agriculture. Mano-ka-lani-pō was *aliʻi nui* in the fourteenth century, the first to rule over a united Kauaʻi after his father Kūkona had defeated the ruler of Kona. It was under Mano-ka-lani-pō that the division of Kauaʻi into *ahupuaʻa* with carefully defined boundaries was begun and great areas of land were opened for agriculture. Kauaʻi is often referred to as *Kauaʻi o Mano-ka-lani-pō* in chants and legends, for his reign is considered the Golden Age of island history.

Between Kamo'okoa and the sea, the Kīlauea River flows across a fertile plain. At the time of the Māhele in 1848 a man named Kealawa'a made a claim for land he had once cultivated with sweet potatoes. Within two years, Kealawa'a abandoned his claim, saying, "The land is being filled with cattle and I have no desire to combat them." Cattle had been brought to Kaua'i by Captain George Vancouver in 1791. They were set ashore with a strict taboo on them to insure their safety. The cattle went wild, and as they multiplied they caused a great deal of destruction to plants and land. The last of the wild cattle were shot in 1939.

The *ahupua'a* is fronted by a long beach unprotected by any reef. Dominating the shoreline is a volcanic cone open to the ocean. Near the top once stood three huge stones that have since been moved, with great difficulty, to make room for sugarcane. These three stones, sisters of great beauty, were a warning that Pele, the volcano goddess, was not to be trifled with.

Pele had come to Kaua'i and fallen in love with Lohi'au, a chief of Hā'ena. She promised to find a home for the two of them, but whenever she struck her staff she was met by water, for her sister Nā-maka-o-kaha'i, goddess of the sea, was her enemy. Pele caused an eruption here, but it was soon extinguished when the sea goddess broke down the walls of the crater, drowning the fire with the ocean. The laughter of the three beautiful sisters enraged Pele. They had seen Pele defeated and shamed. Their scorn was not to be endured. "What are your names?" Pele asked. And one replied, "I am Kalama, this is Pua, and this is Lāhela." Pele repeated their names, touching them with her staff as she did so, turning them to stone. They were a mute and visible warning to all who saw them not to laugh at or ridicule Pele.

It is also said that Pele met Kalama, Pua, and Lāhela on the slopes of Kīlauea Crater. Because they were very beautiful, Pele immediately grew jealous of them. She was afraid that if Lohi'au saw them he would fall in love with them. To prevent this, she turned the three sisters to stone. Then she continued on her search for a home for herself and her lover.[19]

Moku-'ae'ae, "fine or small island," is a 104-foot-high rock islet just off the crater. The Menehune, when they first were circling and exploring the island, tried to bridge the channel between this island and the mainland with rocks. Just as they were able to touch bottom with their paddles, daylight interrupted their task. Because the Menehune never went back to finish a job they hadn't been able to do in one night, the causeway was never completed.[20]

Halele‘a District

Napali

Ko‘olau

West Kona

Puna

East Kona

*H*ale-leʻa, "house of happiness," has always been cited in chants as the most beautiful place in all the islands. It stretches to the sea from Waiʻaleʻale in the center of the island and borders the district of Nāpali on the west. On the east it is separated from Puna by the Makaleha Mountains and from Koʻolau by an open plain. The seashore contains the largest reefs of the island and the only true lagoon.

Its many rivers irrigated extensive lands with rich soils, ideal for taro, which grows in pond fields. Sloping plains, suitable for dryland farming, lead to mountains that soar 4,000 feet or more above the sea. Abundant rainfall meant the land was able to support a large precontact population. Carbon dating indicates that a complex irrigation system for wetland farming was fully in place by 600 A.D.

Before Western contact in 1778, the rolling plains were covered with open forest of native trees, such as the *kou* and *milo*. There were several well-known groves of *hala* whose sawtoothed leaves are used to weave mats. Beneath the trees was a carpet of grass and occasional shrubs and vines. Surviving place-names indicate where many of the endemic plants grew, for they were easily seen; the junglelike appearance of Haleleʻa today can be attributed to introduced post-contact plants.

Haleleʻa is cooled by the Kaiāulu, the pleasant and gentle trade wind. Sometimes the Hao-Koʻolau-o-Haleleʻa, "Koʻolau trade winds coming with force," blows, an unfriendly reminder of the power of nature.

Kalihiwai

Ka-lihi-wai, "water's edge," is the fourth largest *ahupuaʻa* of the Haleleʻa District, containing 8,600 acres. Kalihiwai borders six other *ahupuaʻa* as the boundary follows the mountain ridge watershed along the peaks of the Makaleha Mountains. It shares a broad plain on the east with Kīlauea *ahupuaʻa* and another on the west with Kalihikai. The Kalihiwai river cuts deeply down the center of this plain, which is cut in two crossways by the ridge **Hale-one**, "sand house." Between

Haleone and the sea is a shallow valley, lined with low, steep cliffs. In ancient times, only this shallow valley was cultivated. At the sea there is a small, deep bay edged by steep-sided headlands.

Hana-pai, "lifting (perhaps as by waves) bay," is a small bay on the west that was the canoe landing place. It is protected by a reef, and the name itself may indicate the lifting of canoes out of the water for storage in *hālau* (sheds) built to store them. **Kai-halulu,** "thundering ocean," is the narrow strip of beach on the eastern side of the river mouth. Its name indicates the rumblings of winter breakers crashing against the rocks.

Kalihiwai is cooled by the wind Na'ena'e-pāmalō-o-ka-hale-'ala, "dried *na'ena'e* blossoms of the fragrant house." The *na'ena'e,* a member of the daisy family, is one of the few aromatic plants endemic to Kaua'i. Fragrant plants were often beaten into *kapa* designed for a chief or a chiefess. The perfume, which arose as he or she moved, clearly announced the rank of the wearer.

The last *heiau* built on Kaua'i was **Kīhei,** named after an envoy of Kamehameha. Having attempted to invade Kaua'i twice and failing both times, Kamehameha decided that diplomacy might gain him the island. He sent Chief Kīhei in 1809 to Kaumuali'i, ruler of Kaua'i. Kaumuali'i showered so many gifts on Kīhei that he decided to remain on Kaua'i. As a reward, Kaumuali'i gave Kīhei a wife and made him the permanent *konohiki* chief of Kalihiwai. Kīhei built a *heiau* to commemorate his good fortune. After he died, the floor of the *heiau* was dug up and Kīhei, ceremonially laid out in his canoe, was buried there. Kīhei's wife, Kekaululu, claimed a houselot and three taro *lo'i* in the Great Māhele of 1848.[1]

Kalihikai

The *ahupua'a* of **Ka-lihi-kai,** "ocean edge," has no large stream draining its land, one of the few on Kaua'i. The boundary, shared with Kalihiwai, begins at the sea, climbs a low headland, and crosses the plains to a low ridge leading to the highest point of the *ahupua'a*, **Ka-paka**, "rain drop." From there the boundary descends across the plains in an arbitrary fashion to another headland and across the sands through a channel in the reef that divides Kalihikai from Hanalei.

Most of the land is a rolling plain that has been gouged by small streamlets which, for the most part, drain away into the neighboring *ahupua'a* of Kalihiwai and Hanalei. The plain drops over low hills broken by four little gulches onto a flat strip of land. It was here that the *lo'i* (irrigated ponds) were dug, taro grown, and the people lived. Along the entire front of Kalihikai is a sandy beach and a wide, shallow reef. The *ahupua'a* contains 2,363 acres.

Hanalei

What is called Hanalei today once consisted of four *ahupua'a*: Hanalei, Wai'oli, Waipā, and Waikoko. Usually the translation of **Hana-lei** is given as "crescent bay," but "wreath making" and "*lei* valley" are closer to the original.[2] The wreaths are the rainbows that appear in the upper valley from the constant rainshowers.

The eastern border begins at a channel in the reef shared with Kalihikai. It then crosses a wide plain broken with small streams to Kapaka. The border continues to Wai'ale'ale at the roof of the island before it joins that of Lumaha'i. Then it plunges across Hīhīmanu and down the ridge of Kamo'okoleaka. From here the border follows no geographical feature but goes straight to the sea across the swampy plains.

Hanalei was justly celebrated for its rains, especially Ka-ua-loku-o-Hanalei, "soaking rain of Hanalei." Hehi-pua-hala, "stepping upon pandanus flowers," is a rain associated with **Po'o-kū**, "erect head," a hill on the cliffs above the river where a large *heiau* once stood. The plains here were once covered with pandanus trees. Lena, "yellow," a yellow-tinted rain, suggests the phenomenon of rain falling in the sunshine. Ka-ua-hāʻao, "gentle rain," fell over Hīhīmanu, so called because its showers follow one another like members of a chief's retinue that came in procession in sections or divisions. Kū-ʻula-o-ʻAnini, "red Kū of ʻAnini," is a rain favored by fishermen. There usually was a *koʻa* (rock pile or cairn) near the sea where fishermen would pray to Kūʻula, their special god, before going fishing and, on their return, leave an offering of the first fish caught.

Hanalei's winds could be beneficial or harmful. At **Hanalei-iki**, "small Hanalei," just above the river mouth, a gentle wind blows called Hau-kaʻeʻe-o-Hanalei-iki, "dried up dews of Hanaleiiki." Life-giving winds were Hau-mu, "silent dew," and Hau-ʻōmaʻo, "green dew," or Lū-hau-o-Hanalei-uka, "scattered dews of upland Hanalei." When the Līhau-o-Lanihuli, "gentle cool rain of Lanihuli," blew, fishermen considered it a lucky omen and went to river or sea.

Not so kind were the winds ʻŌ-lau-niu-o-Puʻupoa, "coconut-leaf-piercing wind of Puʻupoa," and Pae-hahi-o-ka-iholena, "row of trampled *iholena* banana trees."[3]

Most of ancient Hanalei lies in the deep, narrow valley along the mountain wall that stretches from the summit of Hīhīmanu to **Wai-ʻaleʻale**, "rippling water," the lake at the top of the island. The water of Waiʻaleʻale flows naturally into the Hanalei River. But long ago, Kalaulehua, a chief of Waimea, brought the Mū people from the floating island Kānehūnāmoku to dig a channel from the lake so that its water would flow into the Wailua River. This the Mū refused to do, and Kalaulehua banished them into the Alakaʻi Swamp.[4]

The *heiau* Ka-ʻawa-kō, "dragged along ʻawa," is located on the south shore of the lake. The *kilo iʻa* (fish watcher) of the Mū would go to Kaʻawakō at the completion of an *ʻoʻopu* fish trap. Here he would make a shrine, present an offering of *ʻawa*, bananas, and *kumu* taro. Then he would make a cup of *olonā* leaves and would chant. This completed the ritual over the fish trap, which he then would close and the fish would be caught.

Near the lake is the peak **Haehae-ka-manu-a-Kāne'alohi-ke-'ale-mai-nei-ka-wai**, "tear the bird, Kāne'alohi, for the water is rippling," on the edge of a high cliff just above the waterfall **Halulu**, "rumbling." Kāne'alohi, a bird catcher, lived in this part of the mountains with his nephew Lauhaka. Their camp was on the cliff side of the Alaka'i Swamp beside an open bit of water. The water of this pool rippled whenever anyone stepped into the swamp miles away. Inadvertently, they were breaking the new rules of Ka-lā-kāne-hina, the Waimea chief, who had forbidden the catching of 'ua'u birds, the dark-rumped petrel, which was good eating. Kalākānehina sent some warriors to kill the two birdcatchers, but they were warned by the rippling water as they broiled a petrel over their fire. Lauhaka called out to his uncle to tear the bird apart so they could eat it before the warriors reached them—hence the name.[5]

Hīhīmanu, "manta ray," one of the three massifs overlooking the valley, has 2,487-foot-high twin peaks that dominate the skyline, so named because the peaks resemble the fin tips of the manta ray as it glides along the ocean surface. These mantas were once numerous along the Nāpali Coast.

It is still possible to disagree on the correct name of a place. 'Anini is an 'ili of Hanalei that shares a reef with Kalihikai. Does this **'Anini** mean "stunted or dwarfish," after the tree 'anini, a small tree that occurs more often as a shrub, or is the name **Wanini**, "pouring water"? The first road sign read *Wanini*. Walter Sanborn, born and raised in Hanalei, was irate because the name had been misspelled, so he shot off the *W* with his shotgun. Therefore people started calling the area Anini because they thought the gunman had corrected the spelling. Many old-timers say that the sign was a misspelling of the true name, **Wai-nini**, "spilled water," from the places in the cliffs where water seeps from the rock face. They claim that neither Wanini nor 'Anini has any meaning as far as this land goes. The debate continues, sometimes with considerable heat.[6]

HĪHĪMANU

Ka-mo'o-o-ka-muliwai, "lizard of the river," was a *mo'o* that guarded the river crossing. He refused to let Hi'iaka cross the river on her way to Hā'ena to get Lohi'au for her sister Pele, and sent freshets of water to sweep her off her feet. Hi'iaka struck him dead, and since that time it has not been as difficult to cross the river.[7]

Hanalei was the home of Kauahoa, a warrior who lived about 1690. He was the last of the great giant *kupua* warriors, noted for his strength, his size, and because he was handsome. He was born on the same day and in the same place as the future ruling chief, 'Aikanaka, and his cousin Kaweloleimakua. In the war between these two, 'Aikanaka did not immediately call upon Kauahoa, who angrily sat in the headwaters of Hanalei River and dammed up the water for so long that the fish gasped in the dry bottom. After he was summoned, Kauahoa tore up a *koa* tree to use as a war club. He did not trim the

WAIʻOLI

NĀMOLOKAMA

branches from the trunk and as he trudged along, birds perched in the branches and sang. Kauahoa and Kaweloleimakua met on the battle-field in combat. Kauahoa struck with his war club, but Kawelo's wife threw her *pikoi* (a tripping club) and deflected the blow. Kawelo then struck Kauahoa and killed him. Kauahoa is often referred to as Ka-me'e-u'i-o-Hanalei, "handsome hero of Hanalei," and this name was given to a headland in his memory.[8]

Wai'oli

Wai-'oli, "joyful water," begins at a point above Nāmolokama Mountain and contains 3,350 acres, an area of great beauty. The massif that dominates the landscape is **Māmalahoa**, 3,745 feet high. Māmalahoa was the wife of Kāne, the supreme god of ancient Kaua'i, and it is most likely the massif was named in her honor.[9]

The middle massif is **Nā-molo-kama**, "interweaving bound fast." After heavy rains, as many as twenty-three waterfalls flow down its face. Its wind is Ua-lani-pili, "rain of the near heavens."

Maka-ihu-wa'a, "eyes for the canoe prow," is a ridge rising from the Wai'oli River. Menehune fishermen complained that on dark nights they could not find their way back to land when fishing on the deep ocean. Their chief devised a plan. He ordered his men to dig out a platform halfway up the ridge and place large torches there. On a dark night the light from these torches could easily be seen from outside the bay. In this way, the first lighthouse in Hawai'i was built.[10]

When the New England Congregational missionaries Samuel Whit-ney and Samuel Ruggles brought King Kaumuali'i's son George Hume-hume back in 1820, Kaumuali'i asked them to remain, giving them land in Waimea on which to settle. Within a year, Samuel Whitney had crossed the Alaka'i Swamp and visited this area. Soon after he formed a mission in Wai'oli. Several families from Waimea joined Whitney and named the lands they settled **Betelema**, "Bethlehem." Today the mission house is the second oldest building on Kaua'i.[11]

Waipā

Waipā, "to request to the gods in prayer," **Wai-pā**, "touched water," or **Wai-pa'a**, "dammed-up water," is a small *ahupua'a* of 1,486 acres. It has a broad river plain nestled between the sea and the ridges leading to the massif Māmalahoa. It shares the crescent bay with its neighbors.

The translation "dammed-up water" refers to the frequent building up of a sand bar that prevents the stream from flowing directly into the ocean. This, according to legend, was caused by a chief named Lauhaka. His mother left her husband, Kalākānehina, the ruling chief of Waimea, during the time of the Kona kingdom because of his cruelty. Lauhaka was raised in the mountains by his uncle, a bird catcher. Learning that two bird catchers were trapping the forbidden 'ua'u, the dark-rumped petrel, Kalākānehina sent some warriors to kill them. Lauhaka stationed himself on the steep path where only one man at a time could come toward him. As Lauhaka killed the soldiers, the bodies fell into the stream and dammed up the river.[12]

Two places in Waipā are named after fabulous mythical birds, **Halulu** and **Kīwa'a**. Halulu was the bird that the great god Kāne sent to the four directions of chaos to announce that he was about to create the world. Halulu was also a man-eating bird that could take on human form when he wished. Its feathers were made out of "particles of water from the dazzling orb of the sun," and each feather was tipped by a talon. Halulu captured a hero named 'Aukele and took him to his cave high on a cliff where he had other captives. From time to time Halulu would reach into the cave with a wing and seize a victim to eat. When Halulu reached in to grab 'Aukele, he and his fellow captives cut Halulu's wing into pieces, after which they did the same to the other wing. When Halulu stuck his head into the cave, 'Aukele cut it off. The two feathers taken from the head were called Hina-wai-koli'i, a name passed on to the feathers that rose and fell on the heads of images in answer to a *kahuna*'s petition.

Kīwaʻa was Halulu's sister and helped ʻAukele leave his prison by creating a poʻomuku (a headless rainbow), so called because it contained only three colors: yellow *(lenalena)*, red *(ula)*, and green *(ʻōmaʻomaʻo)*. The kīwaʻa is also the pilot bird that leads a navigator through the surf to the canoe shed at the landing place.[13]

Waikoko

Another small *ahupuaʻa,* the fourth to share the great bay, is **Wai-koko,** "bloody stream." When Lauhaka was damming up the neigh-boring stream, the blood from the soldiers flowed into this stream and colored it red. In ancient times, however, an aquatic plant grew in this stream that dyed the water red, but these plants disappeared when rice began to be grown here.[14]

Both Waikoko and Lumahaʻi, its neighbor to the west, had sinister reputations for being dangerous to travelers. The ancient road crossed the headland **Maka-hoa,** "face of a friend," and descended to the beach **Ka-halahala,** "young stage of the *kāhala* fish." Ka-puaʻa-pilau and two friends lived here, robbers well trained in the art of *lua* (bone breaking). They were *ʻōlohe* (robbers who removed all the hair from their head and body and kept their skin well oiled and slippery). An *ʻōlohe* inherited a fearsome reputation, usually well deserved. One of his friends watched from the ridge. If several travel-ers came together, the lookout called out, "High tide!" and they were not attacked. However, if a single traveler, well laden with goods, came along, the lookout called, "Low tide!" and the traveler was attacked, killed, and his body placed in a hole in the tongue of lava at the foot of Makahoa Ridge. In time, the body was taken out to sea by the waves and brought ashore onto the sands. The *konohiki* of Wainiha was disturbed that so many bodies were coming ashore and sent a man to spy on the situation. This man saw and heard what was happening and reported back to his chief. The chief and his warriors successfully killed the three robbers, and their bodies were thrown into the pit where they had disposed of their own victims.[15]

At the next headland, a path of rocks was built to skirt the cliff against which the waves often times crashed. This is **Ka-hula'ana**, "cliff point at the seashore where one must swim around to the beach on the other side of the cliff." This path washed out anytime there was a storm, which meant a traveler had to return home to wait until the path had been repaired or swim around it in dangerous waters. A chant that accompanies a *hei* (string figure, a popular pastime), says:

Pihapiha, kai o ke alahula,

Piha, lele 'ū.

"The sea path is full,

It is full; jump in."[16]

When Hi'iaka and Wahine-'ōma'o came, Ho'ohila, the *mo'o* who guarded Kahula'ana, caused the waves to smash high against the cliff. She came out of her cave to see what Hi'iaka would do. Wahine-'ōma'o scooped up a handful of sand and flung it into the *mo'o's* eyes. Ho'ohila retreated into her cave, her spell forgotten. The waves died down and Hi'iaka and her friend continued on their way.[17]

Lumaha'i

Lumaha'i is a large *ahupua'a,* still undeveloped, that belongs to the estate of Bernice Pauahi Bishop. The exact meaning of this name is unknown. According to Lyle A. Dickey the name is pronounced as one word, **Lumahai,** so named for a medicinal plant and also a string figure (a cat's cradle). However, Pukui, Elbert, and Mookini *(Place Names of Hawaii)* list the name as **Lumaha'i,** although no meaning is given.

This *ahupua'a* begins as a narrow, high-walled valley far up in the mountains. About halfway to the sea, the valley opens into a broad plain edged with high walls. The river flows directly into the ocean on the west side of the land, where there is a thick black tongue of lava.

There is no reef; the land plunges into deep ocean here and waves crash dangerously against the sand even on the calmest days.

A special wind was Kalena ka makani lawe pua hala ‘ai a ke kīna‘u, "Kalena is the wind that strews the pandanus fruit eaten by kīna‘u eels." The kīna‘u, a small white eel, ate the hala fruit and in turn were eaten themselves.[18]

A man and a woman, students at the hālau hula at Hā‘ena, fell in love despite the taboo on such relationships. They fled just before graduation after they had offered prayers asking forgiveness of Laka, goddess of the hula. Kilioe, who was chiefess of the school, followed them. She caught the young woman at Ho‘ohila's cave and killed her. Then she chased the man up the ridge, where she killed him. The lovers were turned by Laka into the beach naupaka and the mountain naupaka. Each shrub bears only half a flower, and like the lovers they are incomplete when separated. But when they are brought together, the blossoms can be made to form a single perfect flower.[19]

Ka-lua-o-Ho‘ohila, a chiefess who lived about 1600, was one of the seven sacred kite-flying children of Ho‘ohila, and is referred to in chants as one of Nā kihi kapu kama a Ho‘ohila Kawelo, "the sacred ‘amakihi children of Ho‘ohila Kawelo." She became the last wife of the aged Kākuhihewa, king of O‘ahu, then wife of one of his sons and grandmother of Kūali‘i, who became the king of Kaua‘i after the death of Kaweloleimakua.[20]

Rocks called **Ka-‘alele**, "messenger," near the river mouth are noted for their redness. One day a Menehune caught a large ulua (jack fish). The fish tried to escape, but the little man struggled bravely and finally killed it. The man was so badly wounded, however, that his blood flowed over the spot and turned the earth and stones red. This place was given the name of the wounded man.[21]

Ke-alelo-o-Pilikua, "tongue of Pilikua," is the lava leaf on the west bank of the river mouth jutting into the sea. Pilikua was a giant noted both for his size and his loud voice. He would stop every traveler to

KEALELOOPILIKUA

relate the beauties of Kauaʻi before letting them continue. But the people of Lumahaʻi, able to hear every word and unable to leave, got so tired of hearing the same things over and over again that they killed the giant and threw his body in the ocean. The birds and fish consumed all of his body except the tongue, which had grown so tough it could not be eaten, and so it remains to this day.[22]

Maʻina-kēhau is a boulder high in the cliffs. A Menehune stone carver was tired of his job. When he could not get his chief to let him change to something else, he decided to leave and started for the mountains. The konohiki Weli sent his men to bring him back. They overtook him at about the middle of the cliff and he was turned to stone. It is a huge boulder in the form of a man with a gray body and a white head. The name, which may be translated as "sickening of the dews," has come to figuratively mean "man out of breath."[23]

Pā-naʻanaʻa, "protruding dish," is a large, flat rock below a waterfall in the river. This rock was moved here by the Menehune from Wainiha. It was hewed out into the shape of a poi board and placed near the falls of the river. Half of the rock was gray and the other half black. To this day, the wī (freshwater shellfish) come out on the gray side in the daytime and on the black at night. No woman can successfully fish there unless she wears a certain lei of shredded kī leaves or breaks off two ʻōhiʻa lehua branches, crying to the kupua as she throws one to the mauka side and one to the makai: "Eia he mohai a he alana naʻu (e haʻi i ka inoa), ia ʻoe e ka hoʻoluʻe a hoʻolaupaʻi wi o uka nei la, e noa hoʻi iaʻu ka mana nui, mana iki o ke kahawai nei, a hoʻi au me ka hoʻopilikia ole ia, me ka nui hoʻi kaʻu wi ke hoʻi, i ole hoʻi au e hilahila i ka ʻōlelo ia mai he lawaʻa paoa e." "Here is an offering from (she must give her name) to bring forth an abundance of wī, from the small mana and the large mana of this stream, grant that I do not get into difficulty and that the wī will not be shy."

When a man comes to fish for wī, he must take two stones and throw one on the mauka side of the stream and one on the makai side.

He also must break off two branches of *lehua* while saying: "*E noa ia'u ke kahawai nei e nā Menehune, Kini, Lau a lau ka 'oukou kokua ia'u, i nui ka'u wī e ho'i ai i hau'oli ko kauhale, a pa'a no ho'i ka waha o ka po'e waha'a a leoleo'a ho'omahuakala ia'u.*" "Free me this stream, O Menehune, bring happiness to my house and confound those sharp-tongued, loud people who do not believe me." If the rules are followed, the *wī* are abundant and easily caught.[24]

Lumahai had three famous groves of trees: the hibiscus of Maihi, the breadfruit of Weli, and the pandanus of Māpuana.

Ka-hala-o-Māpuana, "pandanus of Māpuana," was a grove of pandanus trees beside the beach. One tree, the transformed body of Māpuana, bore red fruit instead of the usual yellow and was famed for its fragrance. Māpuana was the youngest sister of 'Aiwohikupua. They came to Kaua'i from Tahiti during the time of Ka'ililauokekoa. Their older sisters were Maile-ha'i-wale, "easily broken *maile,*" Maile-kaluhea, "fragrant *maile,*" Maile-lau-li'i, "small-leafed *maile,*" and Maile-lepa-kaha, "*maile* of the striped flag marker." 'Aiwohikupua tried to win Lā'ieikawai as his wife with the aid of his sisters, but when they chose to become her guardians and refused to let her marry him, he deserted them on Hawai'i. After Lā'ieikawai married a Kaua'i chieftain, the sisters returned to Kaua'i with her.[25]

Ka-hau-o-Mā'ihi, "hibiscus tree belonging to Mā'ihi" or "coolness of Mā'ihi," was a grove of *hau* trees. This grove is all that is left of the *heiau* that a Menehune named Mā'ihi-lau-koa began soon after the Menehune arrived at Lumaha'i. First he marked the edges of the *heiau* with stakes of hau wood. Then he began to construct rock walls around a platform of coral. Before the work could be finished, a huge owl named Pueo-nui-o-Kāne, also known as Ka-'ā-'aia-nu'u-nui-a-Kāne, flew overhead. This was a fearful omen and gave rise to a saying:

Papapau kākou he 'ā'aia kō ka hale.

"The legendary bird strikes at everyone."

(Everyone in an *ahupua'a* might be punished by a chief for some real or imaginary offense by imposing a tax so heavy as to be almost impossible to pay.)

The *'ā'aia* was an evil bird that used to destroy people in ancient times and in general caused great misfortune. When, the following day, he saw the supernatural dog Ka-'īlio-niho-'awa within the *heiau* walls, Mā'ihi abandoned his work, as both of these were manifestations of the two great Polynesian gods, Kāne and Kū. Later, the Hawaiians named the *heiau* Ka-'īlio-pā'ia, "fenced-in dog," because sometimes a large black dog would appear to travelers to warn of danger on the road. The *hau* stakes sprouted and became a grove of trees that cast a cool shade, welcoming weary travelers on hot days.[26]

The grove Nā-'ulu-o-Weli, "breadfruit trees of Weli," was planted by Weli, the first Menehune *konohiki* of the *ahupua'a,* described as bow-legged and deep voiced. The hole in which the shoot was planted was dug by Oha-ka-leo, "loving is the voice," who instructed the tree so well on how to grow that it became famous for its huge fruit, which contained lots of meat. The branches also grew close to the ground and gave rise to a saying:

Nā 'ulu o Weli pūnohu mai ana.

"The breadfruit trees of Weli spread out their low branches like clouds."[27]

Wainiha

Wai-niha, "hostile waters," is the longest valley on Kaua'i, stretching some fourteen miles from its top to the sea. The headwaters of its river rise in Alaka'i Swamp, and its name warns of the floods that occur during torrential rains. The river has formed a narrow, steep-sided valley whose cliffs rise abruptly to over 3,000 feet. The valley widens only a little near the sea to a bay that is usually too rough for any ocean activity. Consequently, the border was widened beyond Lulu'u-pali, "heavily laden cliff," to include the long, flat area and reef of Naue.

There were *lo'i* far up into the valley, many of them displaying great ingenuity in their placement and the engineering of the ditches necessary to water the fields. Sweet potatoes for food, paper mulberry for clothing, *olonā* for fiber, *noni* for medicine, and other useful plants were grown the entire length of the valley.

Bananas grew everywhere. One species, the *mai'a* Polapola, the Borabora banana, grew wild. This banana was considered to be indigenous to Kaua'i, but perhaps was brought here by the mythical Mū who lived in this wild valley.

The Mū were brought to Kaua'i by Kalaulehua, a Kaua'i chief, from the floating island Kānehūnāmoku. They lived below the peak **Hinana-lele**, "leaping young goby fish." Banana plants supplied them with their principal food, their clothing, and household needs. They did not know how to use fire. An important source of protein in their diet came from the *'o'opu*, a goby fish. The Mū built a bamboo trap across the river under the direction of a *kilo i'a*, a fish expert who was charged with giving all the proper offerings to the gods. If he failed, a flood would sweep down the valley, taking the trap with it.

Ka-maka-kilo-i'a, "eyes of the fisherman," a peak and cliff near Wai'ale'ale, was named after a leader of the Mū. During his travels around the island, he reconstructed the navigational course that had brought the Mū, secured canoes, and led his people back to their ancient homeland.[28]

Wainiha was famed for the variety and quality of the *'awa* that grew here. *'Awa mamaka*, a variety of *'awa* with short internodes and a light green stalk, was always in demand. The best, *'awa mokihana*, which had a fragrance similar to the *mokihana* berries of mountains, had short, yellow-white internodes and hairlike roots. It gave a particularly potent brew.

Mauna-hina, "gray mountain," is the ridge leading from the Wainiha River to Alaka'i. The major pathway from the Halele'a District directly into the mountains and on to the Nāpali valleys climbed this ridge to Kilohana. At the base of Maunahina was one of the seven villages of Wainiha. There are remains of many house sites here, mostly of the terraced type that measure ten to fifteen feet wide. The trail was originally made under Ola, the renowned Waimea chief.[29]

At Lā'au, "tree," there is a sloping plateau overlooking the river, with a forest of banana trees. A stream was dammed up to irrigate the taro patches. The dirt-walled ditch ran between the rocks that were laid in place. Hō-mai-ka-lani, "bring me the chief," was the Menehune settlement in Wainiha. It was *makai* of Lā'au-haele-mai, "tree that comes by." There are remnants of many terraces—both *lo'i* and house sites—in this area.

Ka-'aluhe'e, "sagging one," or Ka-lau-he'e, "slippery leaf," is a stream on the east side of the *ahupua'a* that flows into the river. On its banks, a lonely young woman beat her *kapa*. She was disfigured with birthmarks and people teased her by saying she was really a *loli* (seaslug). One day, as she beat her *kapa*, a *he'e mākoko* (deep ocean octopus) swam up the stream and settled on a rock near her. She was so lonely that she began to talk to the octopus. After many days, the *he'e* revealed that he was a demigod who could assume the form of a man. He assumed his human form and his face, too, was marked as hers. Loli fell in love. She left her tapa soaking too long in the stream while they dallied. Her scandalized parents tried to separate the lovers, but Loli jumped off the nearby cliff. She was changed into a *he'e mākoko* to be united forever with her lover.[30]

Ka'u-maka, "my eye," the black rock point on the west side of the bay at the end of Lulu'upali, has several stories connected with it.

Ka'umaka-a-Mano's grandfather had united the island into one kingdom and his father, Mano-kalani-pō, had been able to enlarge the cultivated lands. Hunting for the man-eating shark along Nāpali was popular. Ka'umakaamano went shark fishing, and that episode became the basis of the tales told of this point that bears his name.[31]

Two brothers, Wa'awa'a-iki-na'auao and Wa'awa'a-iki-na'aupō, were fishing. The older, who didn't want to clean fish, said that all fish with two eyes belonged to the younger brother, while he, the older, owned all the fish with only one eye. A shark with only one eye (the other was blind and bulged out like a nipple, hence **Ka-ū-maka**, "nipple," a variation on the name) was caught by the younger brother, who immediately turned the line over to his older brother. The shark towed Wa'awa'aikina'auao out to sea where, with great difficulty, he escaped from the shark and returned to land.[32]

Another story of this point concerns two male *kupua* named Ka'u-maka, "my eye," and Ka'u-weke, "my weke fish." They were fishing at this cape, but all the small fish had disappeared. They saw a shark and Ka'umaka jumped into the water and fought with it. Ka'umaka was very strong and killed the shark. Ka'uweke was able to catch *weke* (goatfish) from the headland once the shark was gone. The two feasted that evening, Ka'uweke on his favorite fish and Ka'umaka enjoying dining on the shark's eyes.[33]

Naue, "trembling," is the sandy flatland that stretches from the headland of Ka'umaka to Hā'ena on the west. The reef was teeming, and the flats were covered with groves of *hala* trees whose leaves were woven into mats. The winds can be very strong and winter storms sweep over the beach onto the land. Tsunami, from time to time, wipe the whole area clean. In ancient times, it is probable that people built only temporary structures along the beach for storage and a place to work in the shade.

When Hi'iaka reached Wainiha on her journey to fetch Lohi'au for Pele, she met Malae-ha'a-koa at Naue as he was fishing. He was crippled and unable to walk. He recognized Hi'iaka and prepared a feast for her. The fisherman and his wife led the dancing and chanting of a long song recounting Pele's story, much to Hi'iaka's delight, and in return she restored his ability to walk.[34]

Hāʻena

Tucked against the Nāpali cliffs is the *ahupuaʻa* of **Hāʻena**. Its name is usually translated as "red hot," a possible reference to the strong taboos that surrounded this place. It is bordered by Hanakāpiʻai on the west and Wainiha on the east. Hāʻena is dominated by cliffs broken with a deep valley, **Limahuli**, "turning hand," and a shallow valley, **Mānoa**, "thick." In front of the cliffs lies a flat, sandy plain with dunes along the beach. A reef extends almost the entire length of the *ahupuaʻa* and at one place forms a large lagoon and a bay, **Makua**, "ancestor," and at another the bay and lagoon at **Kēʻē**, "avoidance."

Kauaʻi's only lagoon, **Kai-kuaʻau-o-Hāʻena**, "lagoon sea of Hāʻena," protects Makua Bay. **Papa-loa**, "long reef," encloses the lagoon. A fishing hole near shore is named **Ka-ʻaulama-poko**, "light from a short-burning torch," because it can be fished at night using a kukui nut torch, which never burned for very long. **Ka-lua-ʻāweoweo**, "ʻāweoweo hole," is the fishing hole at the farthest point from land. The *ʻāweoweo* (bigeye fish) gather in this grotto. It is a twenty-inch-long fish having white flesh. It was eaten raw, cooked, or dried. A large school of young *ʻaweoweo*, called *ʻalalauā*, swimming into a bay was an omen of the death of a high chief.

On the way to Kauaʻi, Makani-kau, chief of the winds, god of love, crossing the channel between Oʻahu and Kauaʻi in his wind form, saw some people in a boat chased by a big shark. He leaped on the canoe and told the frightened people he would play with the shark and they could stay near without worry. Then he jumped into the sea. The shark turned over and opened its mouth to seize him, but he climbed onto it, caught its fins, and forced it to flee through the water. He drove it to the shore and made it fast among the rocks. It became the great shark stone, **Koa-manō**, "shark warrior." Paʻihulu of this century, needing to travel to Kalalau, would come to this rock and offer prayers and food to a shark. The shark would then carry the *kahuna* to Kalalau and back again.[35]

Hā'ena was always ruled by a chiefess and remained politically independent of the *ali'i nui*. The chiefess was in place for life, unlike other *ahupua'a* chiefs who served in their ruler's name and lost their positions when a new ruler was named.

After his second failed attempt to invade Kaua'i, Kamehameha sent several envoys, one after the other, to persuade Kaumuali'i to submit to his sovereignty. The first few envoys were greeted warmly and given land and material wealth. One of these was the high chiefess Kekela, who was offered Hā'ena—which she took, never returning to Kamehameha. She was still alive for the Mahele in 1848 and directed the people to file their claims for land.[36]

Monk seals were often seen here and were called *'īlio*, perhaps because the bark of seal and dog are similar. Hā'ena was noted for the quality of dog that was grown here as food for the chiefesses who were not permitted to eat pork.

Ke-a'a-lewalewa, "dangling root," is a peak on the east side of Mānoa Valley. *A'a lewalewa* are the aerial roots of the *'ōhi'a lehua* tree of the forests or the pandanus tree of the lowlands. Kea'alewalewa was a Wainiha man who constantly stole food from the Menehune farmers in Mānoa Valley. They got so angry after a time that they chased after him and turned him to stone. The name conveys the connotation of "dangling," and thus indicates that he was doing more than stealing food.[37]

Another Hawaiian man and his wife used to steal from the fields of the Menehune farmers in Mānoa Valley. The Menehune finally chased after the two with intent to get rid of them once and for all. They chased the wife into Limahuli Valley. Near the waterfall, she had to stop for she was too tired to run farther. She was out of breath and sat gasping. The Menehune caught her there and killed her. She was turned to stone and is called **Naenae**, "congested." The man was chased up the ridge toward Pōhaku-o-Kāne. He was frightened, but he was very strong—as well as twice the size of the Menehune—and he put up a strong fight. The Menehune used their slingshots and pelted him with stones. Some of these were so large that the bones of his skull were shattered and stuck up through the scalp. In this form he turned to stone, and the ridge where he lies was named **Ka-iwi-ku'i**, "hammered bone."[38]

Nā-piliwale, "clinging ones," a stone formation on the Mānoa ridge, looks like two running figures with their skirts flying up behind them. It was the custom of the four Piliwale sisters to visit a chief's court and remain until all the food in the area had been consumed. Therefore, their appearance heralded a forthcoming famine. They had prodigious appetites and their favorite foods were the freshwater shrimp, the *wī*, freshwater snails, and the fiddlehead of the fern *hō'i'o*. Two of these sisters came to Hā'ena for a visit. Because they were *kupua* and could not tolerate the sun, Lohi'au and his sister Kahua built them a shelter in Maniniholo Cave and another on the ridge where they could enjoy the view. They were fed their favorite foods all through the night and were entertained by every hula dancer of the school at Kē'ē. As the night winds grew chill, Kahua ordered the sides of the shed enclosed with mats. The sisters so enjoyed themselves that they forgot the time. Then at dawn Kahua drew aside the wall coverings and the sisters, with cries of dismay, raced down the ridge to the cave. The sun's rays caught them as they ran and they turned to stone. They remain there as a warning to the other two sisters not to visit Kaua'i.[39]

Kaiwiku'i Ridge contains a large cave, **Manini-holo**, "traveling reef surgeonfish." Maniniholo was the head fisherman at the time the Menehune were leaving the island to return home. He brought his workers to gather food from the reefs and bay of Hā'ena, but there was so much that they left some behind. During the night, all this food disappeared. Maniniholo saw little *'e'epa* (imps) in fissures of the *pali* and realized they were the thieves. He and his workers dug into the stone and killed all the 'e'epa. The cave was named after the head fisherman. The Menehune gathered in the mountains and crossed Nāpali, eventually coming to the plain in front of Maniniholo. There they boarded their canoes that were waiting for them in Makua Bay. They sailed away and never returned.[40]

'O'o'a'a, "fast-rooted one," is a boulder formerly on Hauwā reef that now lies in the depths. 'O'o'a'a came to Kaua'i with her two brothers in the form of rocks. After their long journey, she rested on the sea and became guardian of the reef. 'O'o'a'a was moved from the reef by the 1946 tsunami. She is still waiting for her brothers offshore and can be seen by snorkelers. **Pōhaku-loa**, "long rock," 'O'o'a'a's brother, rested on the top of the sand dunes, leaving his brother Pōhakuokāne to continue alone. **Pōhaku-o-Kāne**, "stone of Kāne," tried to climb to the peak above but, as he was a round stone and the cliff was sheer, he always failed the final climb up the cliff and rolled back to the bottom where he would start over. The god Kāne took pity on him, reached down, and placed the rock on the peak. It is said that when Pōhakuokāne decides to leave his perch, Kāne will raise the waters of the ocean to his level.[41]

Makana, "gift," is a triangular peak, prominent and unmistakable. Firebrands, which were pieces of *hau* or *pāpala* wood whose core was soft and so burned before the outer layers, were thrown from the top of this peak. Under the right conditions of wind, the brands would fall and rise and slowly move out a mile or more over the sea, leaving a trailing glow of embers. On the side of Makana is a storied stone, a reminder of a tale of friendship.

Nou had always dreamed of throwing a firebrand. Once Nou followed the firebrand throwers up the mountain but, being a boy, he was left far behind. He saved the life of a Menehune who had fallen and was caught by the foot on the edge of a sheer drop. In return the Menehune promised Nou he'd become a champion thrower. When Nou threw his firebrand, the Menehune puffed and blew the brand far out to sea. It was a magnificent throw and won the prize offered by the high chief. Jealous, the firebrand throwers killed Nou. The Menehune put Nou's body in a cave and sat at the entrance and allowed himself to be turned to stone to guard the bones of his friend.[42]

Kanaloa was one of the four major Hawaiian gods, the brother of Kāne. The two were noted for digging sources of drinking water as they toured the various islands. The upper wet cave was dug by him and it is called **Wai-a-Kanaloa**, "water made by Kanaloa." Other legends say it was Pele who struck the cliff here with her staff Pā'oa when she was searching for a home, but was met by water instead.

Hala-aniani, "clear pandanus," the lake of fresh water within the cave, was set aside for the *ali'i;* commoners could not bathe in it. The waters were thought to be able to restore an ailing person back to health. The chiefs either drank from a calabash filled with the water, or—better—swam in the underground lake.[43]

Pā-ka-moi, "enclosure of the threadfish," a boulder near the base of the upper wet cave, is also connected to the story of Pele and Lohi'au. When Hi'iaka and her companion Wahine'ōma'o reached Hā'ena, they asked Pākamoi, a fisherman, to find them a place to sleep for the night. He mistook the tenor of their request and after watching them loosen their clothes in preparation for sleeping, he attempted to fulfill his desires on Hi'iaka. Hi'iaka was saved by Pā'ū-o-Pala'e, a friend and servant, who changed places with her. Pākamoi was turned into a stone where he lay.[44]

The lower wet cave is **Wai-o-ka-Pala'e**, "water of the lace fern." In olden times, the water in this cave had a brownish cast, which was said to be the hair of a beautiful *mo'o* maiden who could usually be seen sitting near the entrance of the cave combing her hair. A chief from Wainiha fell in love with her and the two disappeared for several months. Then the mermaid reappeared with a baby at her breast. When asked where the chief was, she drew a finger across her neck to indicate he was dead. In revenge, his friends tried to kill the *mo'o*, but she dove into the water and escaped. Her long hair spread out in the water, giving the pool its colored cast. As she grew older the brown tint turned gray. For this reason, the cave was known either as **Wai-a-kapa-lae**, "water of terror," or as **Wai-a-kapa-la'e**, "water of shiny tapa."[45]

The beach and lagoon at the beginning of Nāpali District is **Kē'ē**, the site of the legend of Pele, Lohi'au, and Hi'iaka. Pele came to Kē'ē when she first was looking for a home and safety from her sister Nāmakaokaha'i. Then, once she had found her home on Hawai'i, she was lured back to Kaua'i by Lohi'au's drumming. She returned to find him and fell in love with him. But each time she dug a cave to make a home for them, she met with water. She left Kaua'i, as she was in her spiritual body, promising Lohi'au she would return for him. After a long wait, Lohi'au hung himself in despair. His body was placed in a cave above Kē'ē and was guarded by two *mo'o* sisters, Kilioe and Aka. When Hi'iaka and her friend Waihine-'ōma'o arrived as envoys from Pele, they found Lohi'au dead. Hi'iaka killed the two guardians and with herbs and prayers restored Lohi'au to life. She took Lohi'au to Pele. Pele, impatient and angry, had destroyed Hi'iaka's *lehua* forest. Equally angry, Hi'iaka embraced Lohi'au. Pele furiously covered him with lava. Hi'iaka dug a tunnel from the sea to her sister's fire pit and almost succeeded in killing Pele before her brothers persuaded her not to. Hi'iaka returned to Kaua'i. Her brothers restored Lohi'au to life once more and sent him after Hi'iaka. The two married and spent the rest of their life together at Kē'ē.[46]

The body of **Kilioe** became a furrowed rock beside the sea that is still used as a birth rock, a place for the safeguarding of the umbilical cord of a newborn. In so doing, the child was placed under the protection of Kilioe. The ancients believed that the fate of the umbilical cord foretold the child's life.

Hā'ena was famed for its schools, where students came to study the sacred forms of *hula* or to learn the history and genealogies of the

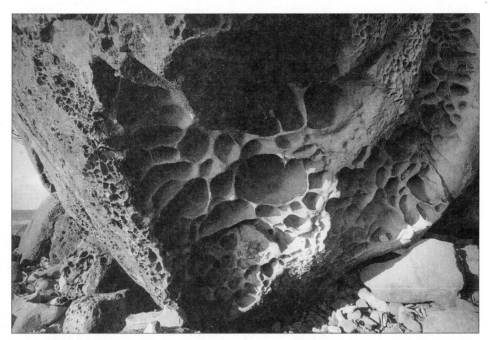

KILIOE

KAULUOLAKA

chiefs. One was **Ka-ulu-o-Laka**, "inspiration of Laka," which contained the school for *hula*, chanting, and composing religious chants, as well as songs. The student remained seven years. The *heiau* and the students were dedicated to Laka, goddess of the forest and dance.

The other was **Ka-ulu-o-Paoa**, "inspiration of Paoa," the school for historians and genealogists. It was said that during the final examination a student listened to a genealogical list that lasted several hours and had to repeat it without error.

Paoa was the *kahuna nui* and close friend of Lohi'au at the time of Pele's arrival. He swore to avenge Lohi'au's death and confronted Pele at her home on Hawai'i. Pele, assuming her most beautiful form, beguiled Paoa into living with her for three days. He drowned himself in shame for not having kept his oath.[47]

Nā-hiki, "many arrivals," is the bay beside the two *heiau*. At the end of their training, students at the hula school had to swim the lagoon, go out the channel into the ocean, and come ashore at Nāhiki where, even on calm days, the waves surge fiercely in and out. In so doing they passed the shark that was fed by the chiefess. Those students who had broken any rules were devoured by it. Those who were without fault came ashore safely.[48]

Nāpali District

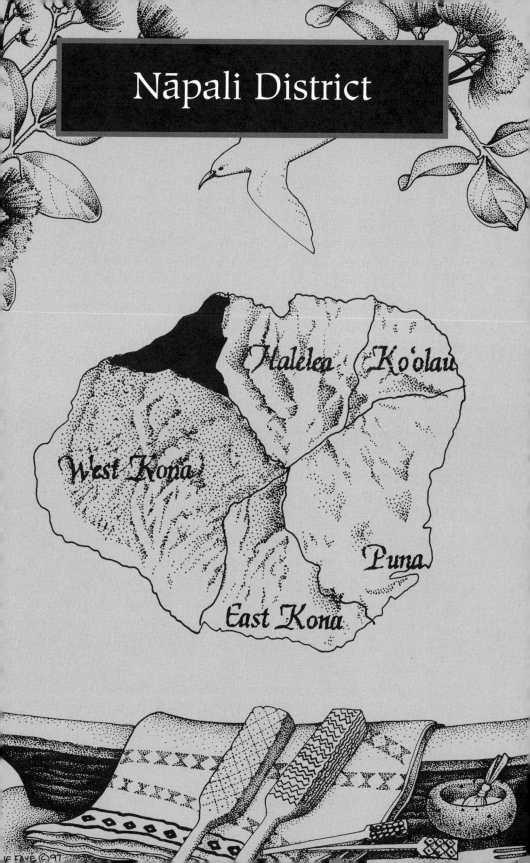

West Kona

Halelea　Koʻolau

Puna

East Kona

*N*ā-pali, "cliffs," is the smallest of the five districts of Kaua'i. It contains seven narrow, short valleys separated from each other by high, razor-edged ridges that rise to an elevation of 4,000 feet directly from the sea in steep, sharp cliffs that give the area its name. Waves break into white foam and splash hundreds of feet high on the cliffs. Waterfalls cascade down green cliffs from the mountains above, fed by constant heavy rainfall, the legacy of the trade winds. Some valleys overhang the ocean behind low cliffs, having no apparent access to the sea. A few have beaches, especially during the summer months, and one has a fronting reef.

Nāpali is constantly buffeted by the wind Ka-lawakua, "strong backed," which blows from the mountains with great force and has become a poetic symbol, as in the saying:

Naue Kalalau, pōniu Ka-lawakua.

"Trembling Kalalau, made dizzy by Ka-lawakua."

(An oblique way to refer to an unreasonable anger.)[1]

The upland forests were filled with honeycreepers, brightly colored birds whose feathers were made into magnificent cloaks, capes, helmets, and wreaths. *Kia manu* (birdcatchers), hunted the forests for three months a year trapping birds for their feathers, which were a prized means of paying the required annual gift to the ruling chief.

Nāpali is rich in fishing grounds. The ocean drops off steeply so that deep-sea fish come quite close to shore. The reef of Nu'alolo provided plenty of fish, seaweed, limpets, and sea urchins. The area is famed for its large sharks: the sixty- to eighty-foot nurse shark; the big whites, man-eaters who were chased by the bravest of royal heroes; hand-fed sharks who carried their feeders from one end of Nāpali to the other; as well as the great shark gods themselves.

During the winter, humpback whales, having given birth in the shallow, warm waters off the Kona district, bring their young here to teach them the skills necessary for their survival. The *hīhīmanu* (manta ray) and the *honu* (turtle) swim close to shore whenever a high surf is run-

NĀPALI

ning. If a *hīhīmanu* is spotted during a calm period, fishermen expect rough seas in a matter of a few hours and take their precautions.

Nāpali's valleys were well populated in ancient times. Each has an irrigated system of taro *loʻi*. Wherever there was a ten-foot-square piece of land that was suitable, either a wet or dry field was created. Houses were built on elaborate stone-walled platforms on land useless for agriculture. During calm weather there was trade with the lands of Haleleʻa and Kona, where hard-to-come-by articles could be found. There were many *heiau*, from complex temples to simple shrines. The sheer number of them attests to the large number of people that once lived here.

There was much travel in and out of these valleys. In calm seas, people could swim from Hāʻena to Kalalau in a few hours. Single out-rigger canoes carved from *kukui* trees, armed with paddles and plaited pandanus leaf sails, carried fishermen into the deep-sea grounds or transported goods for barter.

Precipitous trails, well maintained, climbed in and out of each valley. However, the trail from Hā'ena to Kalalau, which is often said to be an ancient one, was actually created in 1860 under the supervision of Controller of Roads Gottfried Wundenberg. He set off over 400 blasts of dynamite. The trail was created in order to bring out coffee and oranges being grown commercially in the valleys of Kalalau, Hanakoa, and Hanakāpī'ai. For this reason the trail was made wide enough for a heavily laden donkey to walk comfortably.

The top of Nāpali is marked by a row of hills stretching from Wainiha Valley to Pu'uokiha. From there to Halemanu, overlooking Waimea Canyon, is the ridge **Ka-unu-o-Hua**, "altar of Hua," which divides Nāpali from the swamps of 'Aipō and Alaka'i. It takes its name from a small shrine in the *ahupua'a* of Miloli'i near the beginning of the Kōke'e State Park. This shrine was built to commemorate the end of the war Ka-welewele-iwi, "stripping of flesh from bones," which was fought in the mid-fourteenth century.

Ka-lau-nui-o-Hua, a ruling chief of Hawai'i island, conceived the idea of conquering all the islands and forming them into one kingdom. He invaded Maui and defeated its ruling chief, Ka-malu-o-Hua. Taking his prisoner with him, Kalaunuiohua next attacked Moloka'i. Shortly thereafter, with the ruler of Moloka'i, Ka-haku-o-Hua, as prisoner, he stormed O'ahu. Here, too, he was successful and captured its ruling chief, Hua-i-pou-leilei. Then Kalaunuiohua invaded Kaua'i. In the battle with Kūkona, who had just united Kaua'i into one kingdom, Kalaunuiohua was defeated and Kūkona found himself in the position to become the supreme chief of all the islands. While deciding what to do, Kūkona took his prisoners on an extended tour of the island.

One evening they camped at Halemanu, far up in the mountains. Kūkona rolled himself into his blankets and pretended to fall asleep. The four prisoners, huddled around a fire, grumbled about their fate and began to plot against Kūkona. The chiefs of Hawai'i, O'ahu, and

Molokaʻi agreed that they should kill Kūkona as he slept and regain their freedom. But Kamaluohua of Maui said, "We must do nothing to hurt Kūkona. Here we are prisoners in his hand and he has not put us to death." Just then, Kūkona rose up from his bed and said, "What a fine dream I've just had! I dreamed all of you were plotting my death but that one," he said, pointing to Kamaluohua. "He defended me and preserved my life."

Ashamed, the four admitted their guilt. Kūkona freed the chiefs of Maui, Oʻahu, and Molokaʻi. He kept Kalaunuiohua until such time as he could be ransomed, since it was he who had begun this affair. However, Kūkona insisted that each of the four chiefs swear to the gods that never again would they or any of their descendants invade Kauaʻi. A small *unu* (shrine) was built and the chiefs made their promise, binding upon themselves and their descendants. This was the beginning of Ka-laʻi-loa-iā-Kamaluohua, "the long peace of Kamaluohua," which lasted until the year 1795.[2]

Place-names of men and women who once lived in or visited these valleys are abundant. Hanakoa and Hanakāpīʻai, who were Menehune chiefesses, died here; Kamaile, who began the firebrand display of Nuʻalolo; Pele, who blasted a home for herself at Hanakoa but was driven away by her sister; Kahua, who first beat the fragrant fern into her tapa; Kamapuaʻa, who visited his exiled parents in Kalalau; Lāʻieikawai, who lived at Honopū for a time; Kiha, who made three voyages to Tahiti—all have left their mark.

Now Nāpali is deserted of inhabitants. There was no one to give new names to the lands where in 1893 Koʻolau the Leper and his wife Piʻilani successfully defied the provisional government's army. Nonetheless, Nāpali's past history, its chiefs and commoners, its sacred places, and its land and streams remain in the place-names.

Hanakāpīʻai

Hana-kā-pīʻai, "bay sprinkling food," was named after a chiefess who died in childbirth on the edge of the cliffs as the Menehune were on their way to Hā'ena to leave Kaua'i. To mourn her death, they remained on the cliffs above the valley long enough to put on a display of athletic games.[3]

A play on words transposes the name into **Hana-ka-pī'ei**, "constant looking out to protect a love affair." A certain chiefess named Hanakoa liked to "make trouble" with a handsome chief named Wai-'ehu. They met in a cave, thinking themselves secure from prying eyes, but brought attention to themselves by constantly peeking out to see if they were observed.[4]

The first headland between Kē'ē and Hanakāpī'ai, at the top of the climb from Kē'ē on the Wundenberg Trail, is **Ka-leina-ka-uila**, "jumping off place of lightning." The cliff that drops from here is **Wai-kā-ama**, "water striking the canoe outrigger." It marks the boundary between Hanakāpī'ai and Hā'ena. Its name indicates the first of many waterfalls cascading down the cliffs, splashing in the sea.

Hanakāpī'ai was famed for its dwarf *'o'opu peke* (goby fish), named *nōpili*. It was one of the *'ai lehua 'o'opu* (lehua flower-eating goby fish), which can climb up a vertical stone jar or wall by slightly moving its suction disk, first on one side, then on the other. It was said to *pili* (cling) to stones and was used in weaning and housewarming ceremonies so that good luck would *pili*. The largest *nōpili* were found in the Wainiha, Hanalei, and Makaweli Rivers, but the Hanakāpī'ai *nōpili* were thicker and shorter. A fat woman was compared to the *nōpili*. So was a short penis, which was also referred to as *'o'opu peke*.[5]

In the 1930s fishermen from Hā'ena and Wainiha would row in a six-oar rowboat to Kalalau to catch *moi* (threadfish). One time, when a man who wore wide-legged *palaka* shorts leaned back on a pull of his oar, his penis stuck out. Another fisherman grabbed it and yelled, "I caught a *nōpili!*" All the men laughed so much that one of them fell overboard. The fish smelled him and swam away, so the fishermen had to row home again empty-handed. But they thought the joke worth the trip.[6]

The wind of Hanakāpīʻai is named Peke, "dwarf or tiny."

Evidently the people of Hanakāpīʻai endured quite a bit of teasing, for they coined a boast:

Ka iki koaiʻe a Hanakāpīʻai.

"The small koaiʻe tree of Hanakāpīʻai."

(One may be of small size but still be as tough and sturdy as a koaiʻe tree, which was prized for its hard, durable wood.)[7]

Hanakoa

The ahupuaʻa of **Hana-koa**, "bay of warriors" or "bay of koa trees," lies between Hanakāpīʻai on the east and Kalalau and Pōhakuʻau on the west and shares a short border with Waimea in the mountains on the edge of the swamp. It has a good deal of gently sloping land on either side of its main stream, as well as in the Waiahuakua drainage basin. Hanakoa has extensive remains of house sites and wet taro terraces extending more than half a mile inland, although many of these sites were obliterated when coffee began to be commercially grown here.

The original name was **Hana-ke-ao**, the name of a Menehune chiefess. When the Menehune were leaving Kauaʻi, they came along the cliffs toward Hāʻena where they were to embark in canoes. Hanakeao, who was pregnant, stepped on a stone that rolled under her foot, plunging her into this valley to her death. The valley was named in her memory.[8]

Hanakoa, Pōhakuʻau, and Kalalau ahupuaʻa of Nāpali are bordered by the ridge of **Manono**, named after an endemic shrub or small tree belonging to the coffee family of plants. It has small purple-green flowers and a bluish black berry. Dominating Manono is the 3,875-foot-high peak **ʻĀleʻaleʻa-lau**, "innumerable white landshells." ʻĀleʻaleʻa are the landshells whose voices, carried by the wind, could be clearly heard on calm nights. The sound resembled the cricket's rasp. Most endemic shells are now extinct, and the few that remain do not sing. They grew at medium to high altitudes and sometimes in bogs.[9]

A secondary valley is **Wai-ahu-akua**, "waters of the altar of the gods," which begins at a summit of 4,005 feet on the Hanakāpī'ai border and whose water flows into the sea. **Wai-la'a**, "sacred water," is the *'ili* at the headwaters of the valley. There are remains of taro ponds and houselots along the upper portion of the stream. No story, unfortunately, accounts for these godly names.

The wind of Hanakoa is Kai-'opihi, "limpet ocean." *'Opihi* are single-shell limpets with a large foot that keeps the animal clinging to rocks pounded by the heaviest breakers. They provided a treat, tasting something like iodized ripe olives, to enliven the bowl of poi. The largest *'opihi* was the *kō'ele*, whose shells were used as scrapers and peelers. This shell was indispensable in the manufacture of *olonā* cordage. Some families considered the *'opihi* an *'aumakua* and would not eat them.

Pōhaku'au

Pōhaku-'au, "swimming rock," is the smallest *ahupua'a*, jammed into a high plain between a cliff-lined shore and the highest peak of Nāpali, 'Āle'ale'alau. On the east is Hanakoa and to the west lies Kalalau. In spite of its size and the fact that it has no beach or reef, Pōhaku'au is rich in legend.

It is named for the rock **Pōhaku-kū-manō**, "rock resembling (a) shark," in the cave **Ke-ao-mau**, "snagged cloud." The rock is sixty to seventy feet long and resembles a shark with its head by the waterfall and its tail toward the sea. The Hanakoa-Pōhaku'au boundary runs over this rock, tradition giving the head to Pōhaku'au and the tail to Hanakoa.

The cave, in the days before the stone appeared, was a favorite place for Ko'amanō, the guardian shark of the seacoast. His *ali'i nui* was Kū-hai-moana. When Laukahi'u, the grandson of Kūhaimoana, came to visit, Ko'amanō took him to visit this waterfall in the cave. They drank deeply of the fresh water and spent the day floating in the sea, feeling the water fall on their backs and listening to the splash of water on the sea, and they were content.[10]

Makani-kau, chief of the winds, flew in his wind shape from his home on Hawai'i to visit Kaua'i. Crossing the Kaua'i-O'ahu channel he saw some people in a canoe being menaced by a huge shark. Taking his human form, he jumped into the sea, climbed onto the shark, and caught its fins. He then drove it to the cave of Ko'amanō and, tying it fast to the walls, turned it to stone.[11]

This stone shark looks so real that even the demigod Kamapua'a was fooled. When he visited his parents in Kalalau with his two wives, they brought him to this cave without telling him anything about what he would see. In the gloom he thought this really was a shark and tried to spear it. His spear chipped off a bit of the rock, and this place is still visible.[12]

Banana leaves were left as an offering to this shark to ask for protection from the dangerous great white sharks that swim here.

Farther west along the coast, a small waterfall trickles down along the face of the cliff. This cascade is **Ka-wai-kū'au-hoe-a-ka-lawai'a**, "water of the paddle handle of the fisherman." Thirsty fishermen still stick their paddles onto the cliff and let the water trickle down the handle into their mouths. Kamehameha, when he attempted to invade Kaua'i in 1795, boasted that he would drink from this waterfall. He never did.

Trails led up and down, following the ridges, for there was no other way in or out of this *ahupua'a*. One resting place was **Ka-ua-ko'ū**, "moist rain," and nearby was **Pueo-inu**, "drinking owl." At another resting place was **Ke-ahu-pōhaku**, "heap of rocks," where the gods used to have sacrifices offered to them.

At the ocean, the headland that divides Pōhaku'au from Kalalau is **Naupaka**, "*naupaka* plant." There are two *naupaka* plants, the beach *naupaka* and the mountain *naupaka*. Both plants bear only half a flower. When a flower from each is brought together, it forms one blos-

KALALAU

som. The two plants represent a pair of lovers separated by death who can be united only by bringing together a flower from each.

Kalalau

There are two possible pronunciations of the name of this valley, and both versions have a story to account for the name. The first is **Ka-lalau**, "the wanderer," named after a giant named Puni who was a great friend of the Menehune and wandered over the island with them. He, with his long legs, could go faster than his friends and whenever they went to Kalalau, he had to wait there for a long time before they came. To pass the time, he began to shape the cliffs into what looked like curtains of tapa to his friends. When the Menehune asked him what he was making, Puni told them to wait until he was finished. Unfortunately, Puni died before he was done and the Menehune never did find out what he was making. But the curtains still remain.[13]

The other version is **Kalālau**, "to seize," and recalls the actions of Kukua-o-Kalālau. He often seized taro fields, fish nets, youngsters, or anything else that didn't belong to him. As he did so, he shouted "'Owā!" This gave rise to the verb *kaikā'owā*, meaning "to seize" or "to take." In time, *'owā* came to figuratively mean "bereaved or forsaken," reflecting the sorrow of those from whom Kukuaokalālau had stolen.[14]

Lani-ku'u-wa'a, "heaven releasing canoe," and Lani-ku'ua, "descended heavens," were strong, fierce winds. Over the centuries, the winds of Kalalau came to stand for anger.

The land between the sharp-edged cliffs and Kaunuohua Ridge is dominated by **Pihea**, "drifted-in," a hill 4,284 feet high that marks the border between Kalalau, Hanakoa, and Waimea. The name refers to the clouds that gather here and obscure the view. Sometimes shouting loudly into the clouds causes them to dissipate for a time so one can enjoy the view.

To the south of Pihea is **Pu'u-o-Kila**, "Kila's hill," 4,176 feet above sea level. The name commemorates Kila, the youngest son of Mo'ikeha. Mo'ikeha chose Kila to sail to Ra'iātea near Tahiti to bring back La'a, his foster son, so that they could visit one last time. Kila endured much hardship due to the jealousy of his two older brothers, but eventually reached Ra'iātea, found La'a, and brought him back to Kaua'i. La'a, ever afterward known as La'a-mai-Kahiki, introduced the sharkskin drum and the rites of the worship of the god Lono. Kila captained the canoe that returned La'a to Ra'iātea, and after Mo'ikeha's death once again went south to fetch La'a so he could collect Mo'ikeha's bones and return them to Ra'iātea. Returning once again, Kila lived in Waipi'o where he saved his two brothers' lives, but disgusted with their treachery, for the fifth time he sailed to Ra'iātea, this time to live out the rest of his life.[15]

Kalalau was not an isolated valley in ancient times. In addition to sea travel, there were at least three trails that climbed up and down the steep ridges.[16]

The most used trail was **Ka-lou**, "the hook." It was a footpath that followed the ridge on the western side of Kalalau Valley, leading from the mountains to the sea. Once men and women could make the climb in half a day.

Kalou begins at **Kilohana**, "vantage point," the flats at the top of Kalalau where Kaunuohua ends. The trail leads to **Nā-wai-a-Lole**, "Lole's waters," a small valley with a spring. It is a good resting place with a refreshing drink of water. The road skirts the top of the valley. A little farther on is **Paka-ua**, "raindrops," where having a raincoat made of *kī* leaves would be welcome. However, in a short time the traveler would reach both **Ke-ana-papa**, "low cave," and **Ka-opuka-ula**, "small red cave," which would provide some shelter from the rain.

Now the path follows along a cliff, **Ke-ala-(a)-ka-'īlio**, "dog's trail," whose name may indicate how the way along the cliff was discovered. The trail descended down a narrow, steep-sided ridge called **Ka-pea**, "scrotum," a possible reference to the fact that the scrotum of a frightened man has a tendency to tighten. Anyone attempting to climb down this ridge is immediately in danger, as the cliffs drop away on either side of an extremely narrow path—a frightening place indeed. At the end of this stretch is **Ka-leina-kākā**, "struggling leap," indicating a dangerous jump.

For a moment, the traveler may rest again at **Ka-puka-ili**, "stony hollow," where **Ke-ana-nui**, "big cave," is located. Nearby is **'Ōhi'a-pu'upu'u**, "rough-skinned mountain apple," indicating edible mountain apples in season.

Skirting around **Lani-ku'ua**, "let down from heaven," a high peak *makai* of the Kalou Trail, there is another dangerous place: **Ka-leina-kolekole-ā**, "leap like a plover's." Once past this danger, the next

NĀKEIKIONĀ'IWI

ridge, **Ka-lau-o-ka-ma'ahea**, "many little breezes," promises a cooling period before the steepest part of the decline, which is yet to come.

First, however, the traveler must pass the fortress **Ka-lī**, "chilly," located in the small valley of **Kapuō**, "call to prostrate oneself before a god or chief." At this point, the road was very narrow with steep cliffs on either side, an ideal place to withstand any aggression by an enemy. Considering Kaua'i's peaceful history, it is doubtful that it was ever used.

At last the traveler reaches **Nianiau**, "straight," the peak that is at the top of three ridges descending precipitously to the ocean. To continue into Kalalau, one takes the right-hand ridge, **Na-keiki-o-Nā'iwi**, "children of Nā'iwi,"[17] which is marked by two large stone pillars on the cliffs on either side of a sharp ridge at the 600-foot elevation.

Nā'iwi's two children, a boy and a girl, could play only during the night because the sun would turn them to stone. They could hear the children in Kalalau below their home playing during the day, and the two children longed to be able to join them. One moonlit evening, the Kalalau children continued to play and Nā'iwi's children joined them. They played all night. Only when the sky was streaked with red did the children realize their danger, and they hurried for home. As they were running up the trail, the sun rose and the children were turned to stone.[18]

Kalou Trail is completely overgrown today and extremely dangerous. The last known people to have climbed up took eight days to complete the journey. Recently, several skeletons of hikers who tried to descend to the valley floor have been found.

Ka-nau, "chewed," was the trail on the eastern branch of the valley along the narrow ridge named **Ka-loa**, "dashed along the way," a fate that overtook an unwary traveler.

Ke-'ala, "pathway," was a trail leading up from the valley on the eastern side. It climbs **Lima-muku**, "short-armed," the ridge from the valley floor to the peak of Ke'ala. The trail continued to 'Āle'ale'alau and down to Kahue Valley in Hanakoa. There was a fortress here, as the path is extremely easy to defend.

The waterfall **Nā-wai-hiolo-mele**, "waters that fall as chants," falls from the land between ʻĀleʻaleʻalau and Pihea, dropping onto a wide ledge before continuing its fall to the foot of the cliff. On this ledge, Koʻolau the Leper and his family withstood the might of provisional government soldiers sent to take them to Kalaupapa, the leper colony on Molokaʻi.

In 1893, to avoid being sent alone to Kalaupapa, Koʻolau took his wife Piʻilani and their son Kaleimanu to Kalalau. When the sheriff tried to arrest him, Koʻolau shot him in self-defense. Troops were sent from Honolulu in a ship. Koʻolau shot one soldier through the shoulder and he fell. During the night, Koʻolau heard him groan. He went down and carried the soldier to the camp and called out to the sentries that their wounded comrade was near. But no one came out of the camp, and during the night the soldier bled to death. Another soldier, in retreating from here, caught his rifle on a branch and shot and killed himself. Both deaths were credited to the "vicious criminal" that the provisional government claimed Koʻolau was. The authorities forced all the inhabitants to leave the valley forever so no one could help Koʻolau. The inhabitants were put on board, their homes were burned, and they were dumped ashore at Hāʻena. Kalalau was never again inhabited.

Koʻolau lived on for a few years more and Piʻilani buried both her son, who also had leprosy, and her husband in this valley. She continued to live alone for several years until she was finally seen and persuaded to return to her former home, where she found that she was a heroine.[19]

In the summer Kalalau has a wide beach, a result of the sand preferring to winter at Lumahai and summer in Kalalau. A large cave facing the beach is **Ke-ana-mawaho**, "cave on the outside," which was a favorite place to camp while catching fish, salting them, and drying them in the sun. On the bluff above the cave was a fish-calling place where a lookout guided fishermen after a school of fish.

A nearby pool of water, **Wai-honu**, "turtle water," provided a safe place to swim. This pool got its name because turtles would lay their eggs in the surrounding sands.

Fresh water for the campers was provided by **Ho'ole'a**, "to praise." The Menehune tried to make an irrigation ditch wall leading from Ho'ole'a to feed taro fields, but the wall broke. After several attempts to repair it, the sun rose and the project was abandoned.[20]

There were at least four *heiau* in Kalalau, in addition to the fish gods of stone or wood with faces carved on them that guarded the fishing grounds. The *heiau* on the ridge west of the first branch valley of Kalalau stream was **Kahua-nui**, "big foundation." Kahuanui, a chiefess, was the sister of Lohi'au, who was beloved by Pele and Hi'iaka, and Limaloa, the god of the mirage at Mānā. She became the head of the *hālau hula* at Hā'ena after Hi'iaka killed Kilioe. Kahuanui was famed for the quality of her tapa. When Pele first came to Hā'ena, Kahuanui made her a tapa into which she had beaten *laua'e* fern, which gave it a delicious scent.[21]

Kalalau was the largest of the Nāpali *ahupua'a*. It was heavily populated, and many remains of house sites and wetland taro patches can still be found. The valley was self-sufficient. The people grew taro, sweet potatoes, bananas, and sugarcane. A variety of taro, undoubtedly developed here, was called *kalalau*. It had a white corm that gave a whitish gray *poi*. *Wauke* and *mamaki* trees were grown to provide bark for tapa that was made into clothing and bedding. Fish were plentiful when the seas were calm. It was a beloved place, for its memory still haunts those whose ancestors once lived there.

Honopū

Hono-pū, "conch bay," contains many house sites and taro terraces fed by an extensive irrigation system. The *pū* is a triton shell with its

HONOPŪ

pointed tip removed that was used trumpetlike to warn everyone that a sacred chief was approaching.

Honopū is said to have produced excellent *olonā* cordage in the olden days. American whaling captains preferred *olonā* ropes to the hemp cordage made in New England. It was stronger and lasted longer. A proverb says:

Ua nīkiʻi ʻia i ke olonā o Honopū.

"Tied fast with the *olonā* cord of Honopū."

(Said of any situation that is made fast.)[22]

The southern beach is **Honopū-wai-kanaka**, "Honopū's water for mankind." The waterfall that falls onto the sand beside the arch is **Kapona**, "variegated colors." The wind is Wai-kuʻau-hoe, "paddle-handle water."

The northern beach is **Honopū-wai-akua**, "Honopū's water for the gods." After her grandmother Waka abandoned her, Lā'ieikawai was adopted by the prophet Hulumāniani, who brought her here to live. She remained for over a year with her companions, the four Maile sisters, while their younger sister, Kahalaomāpuana, searched for a husband for her. Kahalaomāpuana returned to say she was successful and to prepare a welcome. Soon Ka-'ōnohi-o-ka-lā, who with his brother 'Aiwohikupua had come from Kahiki, arrived and married Lā'ieikawai. They moved to Wailua to live. When Ka'ōnihiokalā proved unfaithful, Lā'ieikawai's parents built her a village where she could wait for the man who was destined to be her husband. The parents disguised the village as a mirage, and Lā'ieikawai became "the woman of the mirage" at Mānā.[23]

The uplands of Honopū are dominated by **Ka-ina-manu,** "sound of birds in the distance," a 4,100-foot peak at the top of **Kala-wao,** "to proclaim through the wilderness," the western valley and stream. It joins Kapaka Stream to form the Honopū River. *Kia manu* (birdcatchers) smeared gum made from the resin of breadfruit trees onto branches of flowering *'ōhi'a lehua* trees, a favorite source of nectar for the little birds. The bird would perch on the branch and become stuck. *Kia manu* also trapped birds by stretching nets between trees. A highly skilled catcher could hold a nectar-laden lobelia flower in his hands and catch the long-beaked bird in his fingers as it thrust into the tubular blossom. Birdcatchers operated only three months of the year, leaving the bird population time to rebuild itself.

Down the coast toward Awaawapuhi is another cave, also called **Ko'a-manō,** the shark god of Nāpali. It was one of his homes along the cliffs. An archway leads into a wide lava chimney that opens to the skies. Pele, it is claimed, dug this cave for her home when she came to Kaua'i the first time sometime around 1350 A.D. Her enemy, Nāmakaokāha'i, found her here and with huge waves broke through the cliff in order to drown Pele and put out her fires. Pele fled, destroying the roof in hopes of crushing her enemy.[24]

Nu'alolo

The name of this *ahupua'a* remains in dispute. Is it **Nu'a-lolo**, "brains heaped up," or perhaps **Nu'ulolo** or **Nu'ololo**, whose meanings are too obscure to even guess at? This is the driest *ahupua'a* of Nāpali and it has been extensively studied by archeologists. They have found traces of former inhabitants everywhere in the valley. A carbon dating indicates that a flourishing community existed here as early as 600 A.D.

The reef and ocean are separated from the flats by low cliffs. In order to reach one place from the other, an ingenious engineering project was built. **Ke-alahaka-o-Nu'alolo**, "the ladder of Nu'alolo," led from the beach to the upper farming area around a bluff. It began at the base of the bluff on the east side of the flats and ran for thirty feet or more on a narrow ledge, sharply overhung by the cliff about twenty feet above the ocean. At the end of this ledge a rope ladder led to another ledge about twenty-five feet above it. The bulge in the cliff made the ladder hang out over the sea. The ladder was fastened into four rings cut through the solid rock for that purpose. A protruding stone near the top of the ladder was grooved, probably for the purpose of lowering bundles to the ledge below. From the top of the ladder a series of notched steps and finger grips were cut that led to a narrow trail running up to the top of the cliff. Anyone with vertigo could not climb the ladder.[25]

Ke ahi lele o Kamaile, "soaring fire of Kamaile," refers to the fireworks cliff, **Ka-maile**, "*maile* vine," a round hill above the concave cliffs. Firebrands, in a display called *'ōahi*, were thrown like javelins from the top of the cliff and soared in the air, spewing out embers until the sticks fell into the sea a mile or two offshore.

The javelins were ten to twenty feet long and made of either *hau* or *pāpala* sticks. *Hau*, a tree brought by early Polynesian settlers for its many uses, was cut to length, its bark peeled off and dried until each javelin was as light as a feather. On a moonless night when the wind was right, men climbed to the top of Kamaile and built a bonfire. One end of each javelin was set on fire and they were launched into the air. Carried by the wind, the blazing sticks rose and fell, blazing brighter and brighter as they flew.

Pāpala was harder to get than *hau,* so it was reserved only for the highest chiefs. When dry, it had a hollow core that burned more quickly than the outer shell. As the *pāpala* javelin flew, flame and embers shot out from the center. The wind for hurling firebrands was named Pāpala, "firebrand."[26]

The mountain is named after Kamaile, a chiefess of Nu'alolo who was loved by Kū-pono-aloha. But Kamaile married a stranger from Tahiti, 'Ō'ili-kū-ka-heana, who brought the first 'awa, a narcotic plant, with him. Kamaile became addicted to the drug and eventually her skin became scaly and her husband left her. She uprooted all the 'awa plants and threw them away. Kūponoaloha, to prove his continuing love, caught a firebrand and scarred himself with it. Realizing the depth of his feelings for her, Kamaile married him.[27]

A wind of Nu'alolo is 'Ai-ko'o, "eating away at the support." However, when the Māpu-'ala, "sweet-smelling wind-borne fragrance," blew, strangers were sure to appear, attracted by the fresh scents of the mountains cooling this hot valley. The headland of **Makua-iki,** "lesser parent," ends the *ahupua'a* of Nu'alolo. Here the wind blows from east to west and is called Koholā-lele, "leaping humpback whale," for when it blows the whales come to play in the ocean along the cliffs of Nāpali.[28]

Awaawapuhi

The name **Awaawa-puhi,** "eel valley,"[29] refers to a *puhi* (freshwater eel) named Kuna who, searching for a new home on Kaua'i, swam along the cliffs. He thought the mountains interesting so he slithered up the cliffs, gouging out this valley on his way to the uplands. It was cold

AWAAWAPUHI

and the eel became sluggish and eventually fell asleep. Later a group of people from Kalalau on their way to Waimea came upon this very large eel lying stiff and straight beside the trail. They prodded and poked it and decided it was recently dead and would make them a fine meal. They tried to curl it up so it would fit into a cooking pit, but they could not rearrange the eel in any way. Instead they lined the eel on both sides with rocks, piled firewood on top and set it on fire. This only woke the eel up, and Kuna ate all the people before returning to the sea. The rocks are still there, a parallel line of stones that marks the length of the eel, and the area was named **Ka-lua-puhi**, "eel pit."[30]

Farther along the trail toward Waimea are two flat stones. These are called **Ka-nahuna-o-Kamapu'upu'u**, "biting of Kamapu'upu'u." Kamapu'upu'u was returning from Kalalau with his three dogs and, resting on one of these stones, set his bundle down and had his lunch. The three dogs sat in front of him on the other stone, the larger two dogs on each side of the smaller dog. As he ate his lunch, Kamapu'upu'u fed the smallest dog with pieces of meat and gave nothing to the two larger dogs. The two dogs, who had often saved the man's life and found this behavior ungrateful and unacceptable, killed the man and the little dog went wild in the mountains. This was the origin of the wild dogs of the forest region. The spirit of Kamapu'upu'u went down to Waimea and told his family, who came for his body and buried it in the valley.[31]

Awaawapuhi is a narrow, steep-sided valley extending from the sea to its headwaters on the south end of Kahuama'a Flat in the mountains. There are remains of taro terraces and many house sites on both sides of the stream, ranging from two to four feet high. There are burial caves on the western cliffs.

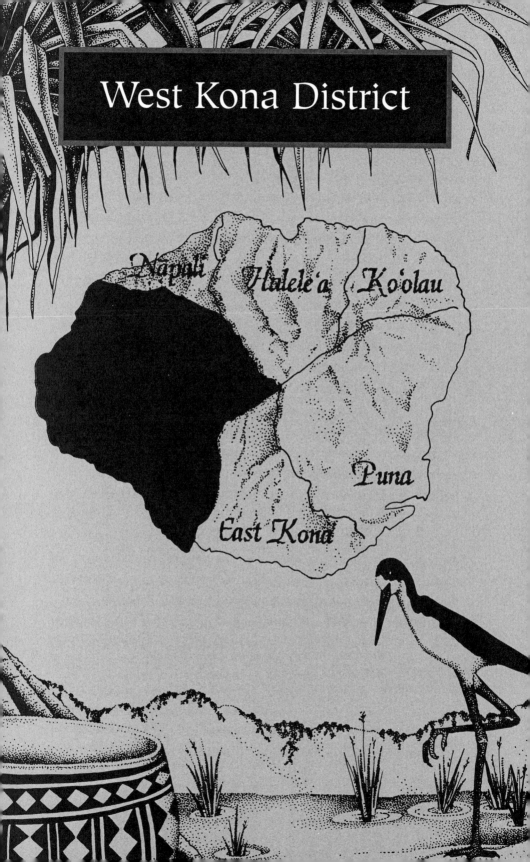

West Kona District

Napali

Halele'a

Ko'olau

Puna

East Kona

Between Nāpali and the Waimea River are numerous valleys and gulches separated by steep ridges that rise from the sea to the edge of the canyon complex four thousand feet above. Once these slopes were covered with *pili* (the bunch grass used for thatching houses), innumerable shrubs and bushes, and groves of trees—*koa*, sandalwood, and the flowering *'ōhi'a lehua,* among others. Most of the gulches had perennial streams that ran with constant water; a few were intermittent and depended for their flow upon the rainfall. There were springs here and there with enough volume and flow to provide for the needs of the people. It was a parklike area of great beauty, even though it lay within the driest part of Kaua'i.

At the foot of the ridges, behind high sand dunes and below ocean level, lay a huge marsh and open pond complex. It was a perfect home for countless birds that provided an easily caught source of meat. Fish were grown in the lakes, and the inventive people built rafts that they filled with dirt and grew taro on floating islands. They lived in little settlements tucked up between the cliffs and the swamp. In the rainy season, it was possible to paddle a canoe from the edge of Waimea town to the sacred precincts of Polihale *heiau.*

With the coming of Captain Cook and those who followed him, these ridges were stripped. Cattle and goats, introduced by Captain Vancouver, foraged freely and ate the grass to the roots. As more and more trading vessels touched shore, they needed firewood and the nearest trees were cut to provide it. When sandalwood was discovered amongst the firewood, it became the major source of income for the voracious Kamehameha chiefs, who now ruled a conquered kingdom with no thought to the future. Soon these ridges were deforested and the soil began to blow and erode away. A fire started early in the twentieth century, and the land itself, rich with rotting leaves, caught fire. The fire smoldered for months. When it was finally put out, the land was barren and eroded, streams and springs had stopped running, and all traces of its former beauty were erased.[1]

156

This area was divided into several *ahupua'a,* but nowadays it is simply referred to as Mānā. Miloli'i maintains its identity because many people say it is part of Nāpali. Wai'awa and Pōki'ikauna have merged their separateness into Mānā, and few realize that **Ke-kaha,** "dry hot place," was part of Pōki'ikauna Beach where the canoes were stored.

Miloli'i

The first of these dry valleys is Miloli'i. It is a narrow valley with steep slopes. The shore is completely lined by reef, still rich fishing grounds. The *ahupua'a* extends to Kaunuohua Ridge in the mountains. The uplands were ideal for bird catchers, as the area is drier and warmer than on the other side of the Kaunuohua Ridge and the forest was not as thick. A small shrine named Miloli'i marked the headland of Makuaiki, the boundary with Nu'alolo. There was an extensive irrigation system, and the remains of many structures, from taro ponds to house terraces, can still be found. These indicate that a sizable population once had ample water for their needs.

The valley is cooled by two breezes: Pāhili-kai, "forceful winds from the sea," and Hā-loa, "long hard breath," which blew from the windward side of **Ke-ana-o-Kū,** "cave of Kū," whose whereabouts is unknown today.[2]

Miloli'i is usually translated to mean "fine twist," a reference to the superb *olonā* cords woven here. *Olonā* cords were used for lashing canoes and houses together, woven into nets, indeed for any purpose needing a long-lasting, extremely strong cord. *Olonā* has long fibers that give it strength. Another possible translation is "small swirling," named after the swirling offshore ocean currents.

Four streams flowed through Miloli'i, but all are dry now except during exceptional rains. These streams, from north to south, are **Kū-kālai,** "Kū the carver," the first stream *mauka* on the left from the sea. Next is **Ka-wai-'ula,** "reddened waters" or "red stream," followed by **Māniania,** "shivering sensation," a steep valley and stream that branches in three in the center of the *ahupua'a*. The name refers to the vertigo one gets from looking down over a great height. Last is **Pā'ā-iki**, "little, dry, rocky area." **Kōpī-wai**, "to sprinkle water," a peak in the mountains, is the watershed of Pā'ā-iki Stream.

Ka'a-hole, "to peel by rolling," is a small valley on the northern end of the seashore. It contained two shrines: **Pōhaku-o-Kāne**, "rock belonging to Kāne," and **Ka-mo'o-ali'i**, "genealogy of chiefs."

On the south is the side valley of **Ka-uhao**, "the scooping." There are house sites here, and near the sea is a platform thirty feet square with walls five feet thick and two feet high. Across a deep gulch from this platform is a small platform. To the east is a paved house site ten by ten feet. Farther back is a three-foot-high wall, ten feet long. Between these is a fireplace for four stones. A cave in the bluff not high above had a wall along its front side. The dryness of this valley suggests that these sites were either temporary fishing shelters or shrines.[3]

The valley was named after Kauhao, daughter of Kapalama and Honouliuli, who lived during the reign of Ahukiniala'a. She married Ke-ahua, a chief of the Puna kingdom, and had two children, Lepe-a-moa and Ka-u'i-lani. The point at the mouth of the valley of **Ka-'auhau**, "tax," is named **Lepeamoa**. She was born in the form of an egg. Her mother's parents raised her on O'ahu. She could take on the form of many kinds of birds as well as that of a beautiful woman, but her favorite shape was that of a hen. Later in life she helped her brother Kau'ilani overcome the king of Maui, thus saving the life of the O'ahu king. She married well and never returned to Kaua'i.[4]

Mānā

Mānā has magnificent beaches, a rich history, many legends and stories, sand dunes that bark like dogs, and a temple that is the gateway to the land of Pō, the dim, twilight land beneath the ocean where the chief Milu rules over the souls of the dead.

This land of sand, marsh, and heat, intermingled fresh and salt water, a land of decorated gourds and of fishermen, the home of super-natural white and black dogs, a land where confused spirits of the newly dead wandered, was not at first a desirable place to live. But a chief named ‘Uwe‘uwele-kēhau and his wife made it so.

They had been unjustly banished from Wailua and sent destitute to Mānā. More and more people joined them as they traveled, and when this large group reached Mānā they quickly created a comfortable home for themselves. When the Wailua chief realized his mistake and pardoned ‘Uwe‘uwekēhau and Lu‘ukia, they refused to leave Mānā. They would not abandon their people who had voluntarily joined them in exile.[5]

Because of the salty marsh between the dunes and the cliffs, the people of Mānā lived a little differently from other folk. When schools of fish appeared, they were caught and canoed to Waimea. People hurried to the canoe landing at Keanapuka with loads of *poi* and what-ever other cooked foods they had on hand to barter for the fish. The Mānā fishermen would place all the *poi* they had gotten in a large con-tainer and pour in enough fresh water to mix the whole bunch all at once. Then they would sit down to a sumptuous meal of fresh poi and fish. Only then would they return home with the rest of the bartered food. *Poi* was a treat, as there were only a few places taro could be grown. The majority of Mānā inhabitants were fishermen and grew gourds wherever there was decent soil.[6]

A long, wide beach covers the western shore south to a point where it sweeps away to the east to the Waimea River mouth. This beach was named **Ka-moena-hohola-o-Mānā,** "unfolding mat of Mānā," by a traveler from Kahiki who lived here. Everyone else on his voyaging canoe had stopped off at one place or another, but only he had the curiosity to see all the islands. He built his house on the dunes so that he could see the beach unfolding before his eyes. When he grew old, he decided to see if any of his shipmates were still alive, and he found a friend in Kona on the island of Hawai‘i. At his friend's suggestion, he

KAMOENAHOHOLAOMĀNĀ

settled down; but in a short time he become homesick for the sight of his beach and persuaded his friend to accompany him back. There he showed off his "unfolding mats," and his friend happily settled down with him.[7]

Where the beach makes its turn on the way to Waimea is **Kapu-ʻai**, "kapu on eating." *Weke* fish caught here have fed on a seaweed that contains a poison that accumulates in the fish's head. This poison can at best cause psychedelic dreams, but can also prove fatal. This still holds true today.

Behind Kapuʻai is a series of large sand dunes called **Ke-one-kani-o-Nohili**, "barking sands of Nohili." As one walks along these dunes, or slides down them, the sound of distantly barking dogs is heard.[8]

Nohili was a fisherman who owned nine dogs. When he canoed out to sea, he tethered the dogs, tying three to each of three sturdy pegs driven into the sand at the top of the dunes. Once he was caught in a terrible storm that blew him almost to the island of Nihoa. The nine dogs barked and barked, first to warn him, then to guide him home. They jumped, turned, twisted, and spun around and around their pegs, constantly barking. When Nohili reached home again, he found no trace of the dogs except great circles around each of the pegs. But as he walked, he heard his dogs barking deep inside the sand where, in their frenzy, they had dug themselves.[9]

At **Kolo**, "creep," "crawl," or "pull," at the foot of one of the ridges that descends from Pu'ukāpele on the canyon's rim, there were five unusual taro patches. During the rainy season, when the marsh filled with water, a framework of wood was made and taken out into one of the freshwater ponds dotted here and there throughout the marsh. Dirt was carried down from the ridges above and poured into the wooden frames until they sank and only the top of the dirt remained above water. Taro was then planted and it flourished. Five rafts were tied together to form one large floating field of taro. Only here and at Hā'ena on the other side of the island was taro grown this way.[10]

The *heiau* of **Poli-hale**, "house blossom," is one of the oldest and most sacred on the island. It is a four-terraced structure. Over the years, the base has been covered by sand and the rest is overgrown with imported weeds. The three outer edges of the first platform have a wall eight feet wide that ranges in height on the inside from one foot along the front to three feet at the junction with the second platform. The wall at each side of the second terrace has a width throughout of eight feet. The third platform measures thirteen by eighty-nine feet, and the fourth measures twenty-one by eighty-nine feet. The facing of the fourth terrace is slightly bowed out, making a curved front. The back side is faced with a five-foot wall and backed by boulders on the slope, which continues upward. The steps of the platform area are roughly finished. The *heiau* is paved throughout. It was built to fulfill a promise.[11]

POLIHALE

Chief Polihale had a daughter, Nā-pihe-nui, who attracted the attention of Kū, the first of the four great Polynesian gods to come to Kaua'i. In the form of a white dog, he would play with her and her maidens as they swam and bathed in the nearby pond. He asked Polihale for his daughter, but he was refused. Kū said he would kill all the inhabitants one by one until Polihale would agree to the marriage. Kū did so in his form as a large black dog. Polihale prayed to Kāne and Kanaloa, two more of the great gods, to help him in this uneven battle. The gods came in their seagoing bird forms and defeated Kū. In thanks, Polihale built this *heiau* that bears his name as the first home in Hawai'i of Kāne and Kanaloa.[12]

At the base of the Polihale cliff is a small spring. By digging in the sand at low tide, a hole can be formed into which fresh water will seep. Formerly this spring is said to have come out in a small cave at the base of the cliff. Both cave and spring were sacred.

The spirits of the dead came to Polihale from all over the island. They gathered at Kā'ana, "divide," on the edge of the canyon where there is a county park and a lookout today. Then the spirits followed the stream Hiki-moe, "to arrive prostrated," down to the *heiau*. Here they rested before climbing to the top of the three-hundred-foot cliff and leaping into the ocean to sink into Pō, which lay just offshore.

Since so many ghosts got lost or wandered about dazed, people who lived in Mānā built their houses with gables facing east and west so that the doors opened to the north or south. Spirits, who seemingly could only move in a straight line, would hit against the gable ends of the house and pass around it, instead of through the door where they would bump against the other inside wall and be unable to continue—and become permanent and unwanted guests.

In the waters offshore grows a sea lettuce called *pahapaha*. Nāmakaokāha'i, goddess of the ocean and sister of Pele, wove a wreath of *pahapaha* when she stepped ashore and gave it a special quality. A *lei pahapaha* can fade and dry out, but when soaked in water will revive to its original freshness. Only the *pahapaha* of Polihale does this. Visitors wore wreaths of *pahapaha* home to prove they had indeed been there.[13]

Kapo'ulakīna'u, another of Pele's sisters, also arrived at Polihale. Here she and her bevy of maidens discovered *kauna'oa*, a parasitic dodder vine, growing in the *pōhuehue* vines along the dunes. The red-orange stems were woven into a wreath, and thereafter anyone who asked Kapo for help in defeating an enemy offered her a *lei kauan'oa*, preferably from the dunes of Mānā itself.[14]

In a cove on the inland side of the dunes, there was a shrine, 'Ele-kuna, "blackness of the freshwater eel." It is a mound of sandstone that appears to be an outcropping. The shrine was built by the

Menehune, which makes it old indeed. On his tour of Kaua'i, King Kalākaua came here to make an offering at the base of the mound. It was one of the things he had specifically requested to do.

Wai'awa

The famous mirage of Mānā, **Ka-waili'ulā-o-Mānā**, belonged to Wai'awa *ahupua'a*. It appeared on the edges of Limaloa Lake in the midst of a large coconut grove called **Kauna-lewa**, "swaying places," named after a navigator on Mo'ikeha's canoe to and from Ra'iātea.[15]

This large and famous coconut grove gave rise to a saying:

A! Loa'a aku la ia 'oe na niu o Kaunalewa.

"Ah! Now you have the coconut of Kaunalewa."

(Your worldly possessions are gone: An impolite saying with a play on *kau-na-lewa*, "hang suspended," as if to say, "Now all you have is a hanging scrotum."[16]

The mirage came with great regularity at dusk. First a series of houses, sometimes as many as seven, would shimmer into appearance, scattered about among the coconut trees. A broad white path of crushed coral led from one to the other until it reached the biggest house of all, the farthest in the back. Then the great chief Limaloa, brother of Lohi'au—Pele's lover and Hi'iaka's husband—strode out of the closest house, dressed in his helmet of yellow feathers and wearing a feather cloak that reached his heels. In one hand he held his spear of *kauila* wood. He strode down the path and disappeared into the large house, where *ka wahine o ka li'ulā*, "the lady of the mirage," lived. Then the mirage would fade away to reappear another night in exactly the same way. It happened on certain nights of the moon, the nights of Kāne, and was so predictable that people would come from other islands to see this phenomenon.[17]

This mirage village was originally built by the parents of Lā'ieikawai, who was a contemporary of Ka'ililauokekoa. She had been born on O'ahu, and as a young girl was taken to Hawai'i where

164

she lived in the mountains guarded by a fierce dragon, Kiha-huna-lūlū-moku. 'Aiwohikupua, a chief attached to the court of Ka'ililau-okekoa, went to seek her for his wife. He took his five sisters with him—the four beautiful Maile sisters and their youngest sister, Kaha-laomāpuana. As it turned out, his sisters thought 'Aiwohikupua was not a suitable husband for her and became her companions and guardians. 'Aiwohikupua returned to Kaua'i alone. After many more adventures with unsuitable men, Lā'ieikawai married, but after a few years her husband fell in love with her twin sister. Lā'ieikawai's parents banished the lovers and built this mirage, where she could await the man whom the gods would someday send. She was called *ka wahine o ka li'ulā*, "the lady of the twilight" or "mirage," for *li'ulā* is both a mirage and the hour of twilight when the eyes are dimmed and the outlines of things shimmer and become indistinct.[18]

Several centuries later, Kapo'ulakīna'u realized that the chief Limaloa, who had so gallantly met her as she landed and had promised to marry one of her young women, was the man fated for Lā'ieikawai. Limaloa's bride-to-be, Moe-hauna-iki, relinquished him and placed his soul within the mirage. There Limaloa and Lā'ieikawai remained for close to six hundred years, until Western commercial interest caused the entire swamp to be drained and the land planted with sugarcane.[19]

When Kūalunuipaukūmokumoku inherited the newly created Kona Kingdom from his father, his *kahuna nui* wished to return to their homeland. In order to discourage the chief, the *kahuna* murdered all Kūalu's sons. Kūalu suspected the priest's involvement in the murders but couldn't prove anything. To insure his succession, Kūalu banished his newly pregnant wife, Kahapula, along with Pi'i, his chief counselor, accusing them of having slept together. Then Kūalu waited until his son grew into adulthood.

Meanwhile, Kūalu sent back to his homeland for the Menehune who were masters of stonework and engineering. At Kūalu's direction, the Menehune built many fishponds and irrigation systems for wet-land farming. They also built many *heiau* and after many years Kūalu ordered them to build a *heiau* in Wai'awa *ahupua'a*. In a natural amphitheater, the Menehune built a huge platform of natural red lava stone and paved it with water-smoothed pebbles and coral. When it was completed, the *kahuna nui* said that it would be necessary to dedicate it with a human sacrifice.

The *kahuna*, who had long wondered about the child of Kahapula, ordered a *kahe* (fish trap) built across the Makaweli River near the home of Kahapula and her son. The *kahuna* placed a *kapu* on the fish trap, but Kahapula's son disregarded the *kapu*, climbed onto the trap, and ate the fish caught there. The *kahuna* caught the boy and took him prisoner to Wai'awa to be the human sacrifice.

Hearing that her son was taken prisoner, Kahapula conferred with Pi'i. He gave her the advice that Kūalu himself had given him many years before: "Take this *malo* (loincloth) and this *lei palaoa* (whale-tooth necklace) that Kūalu gave his son. You must walk from here to Wai'awa and juggle six *kukui* nuts as you go. If you drop one, your child will die. If you catch them all, he will live." Kahapula immedi-ately set out and her attendants carefully cleared the path of all rocks and sticks that might trip her on her fifteen-mile journey.

She reached the *heiau* at Wai'awa, not having dropped a *kukui* on the way. She knew this was a good omen as she went past the guards, who had all fallen asleep. She found her son tied with ropes and released him. The youth, however, refused to run away.

The following morning, the young man was led before Kūalu and the *kahuna* at the foot of the altar. The boy knelt before Kūalu and placed both the *malo* and *lei palaoa* at his feet. Kūalu, with a shout of happiness, lifted his son to his feet. The *kahuna nui*, immediately real-izing the loss of his hopes, tried to spear the youth, who easily brushed the weapon aside. The *kahuna* stabbed himself and thus inadvertent-ly became the first human sacrifice on Kaua'i.

Kūalu named his son Ola, "life," and the *heiau* **Hau-ola**, "live offering" or "dew of life." From then on there was no looking back at a former homeland. Under Ola, the Menehune built irrigation ditches within the Waimea Canyon complex of valleys, turning them into so rich and comfortable a land that even the stories of the former homeland were lost.[20]

Pōki'ikauna

The *ahupua'a* of **Pōki'i-kauna**, "chanting younger brother," lies between Wai'awa and Waimea. It extends from the shore to the peak of Pu'ukapele and is where two ancient legends known throughout Polynesia were situated by local storytellers.

The first of these is the story of Hiku, who was born in the forests of Pu'ukāpele and who owned the magic spear Kani-ka-wī. The day he went to the seashore for the first time, he met Kawelu, a chiefess of Pōki'i, and the two married. Kawelu, ignorant of the niceties of protocol, forgot to offer Hiku anything to eat and after three days Hiku left her and returned to the mountains. Kawelu attempted to follow him, but even the vegetation spitefully resisted her at Hiku's request. Kawelu returned home and hung herself. When Hiku heard this, he was filled with remorse and decided he would go into Pō, find her spirit, and return it to her body. He braided a long vine into a rope and was lowered into the land of the dead, which lay deep underwater off Polihale. There he found Kawelu and persuaded her to join him, swinging on his rope. She was pleased with the game and did not notice when the rope began to be pulled up. The higher the rope went, the smaller Kawelu's soul became, until Hiku was able to imprison it in a coconut container he had created for this purpose. He brought the spirit to Kawelu's body and persuaded it with many chants to reenter her body. When Kawelu opened her eyes once more, Hiku promised never to leave her again.[21]

Punanuikiniakua, who came from the Marquesas and settled on the banks of the Wailua River, was a direct descendant of three men famed throughout Polynesia. The first was Hema, who sailed from his homeland to find a birth gift for his son Kāha'i and never returned. Kāha'i, in his turn, sailed away to find a birth gift for his son, Wahieloa, who also sought a gift for his son, Laka, and never was seen again. Laka lived in Pōki'ikauna and often roved the mountains of Pu'ukāpele. He was teased as a child for being fatherless and when he got old enough, he told his mother he was going to build a canoe so he could find out what had happened to his father and grandfather. He went to Pu'ukāpele and cut down a huge *koa* tree ideal for a voyaging canoe. He left the tree where it had fallen and returned to the shore to spend the night. When he returned the next morning, the tree was back in its place, growing as strongly as ever. Laka cut it down again, and once again he found it restored in the morning. The third time he chopped the koa down, he hid in the branches. During the night a band of Menehune arrived, and when they tried to replace the tree, Laka caught the two leaders by their beards and refused to let them go until they promised that they would carve him a canoe that would safely take him wherever he wanted to go. Laka, as he was bidden, returned to his home on the beach and had a shed built on the sands of Kekaha where the canoe could be finished. During the night the Menehune brought the completed canoe to the shed. Laka set sail, and in time he found both his father and grandfather and brought them home with him.[22]

Pōki'ikauna received its name from a chant sung from its ridge by the youngest brother of Kapo'ulakīna'u. When they left Mānā, the young man chanted a farewell to his sister, Moehaunaiki, and it is this chanting that gives the *ahupua'a* its name.

At the edge of the *ahupua'a*, just before the boundary with Waimea, is the beach **Ke-one-kapu-o-Kahamalu'ihi**, "sacred beach of Kahamalu'ihi." Kahamalu'ihi was a chiefess who lived about 1650 A.D. and is referred to in chants as Ka-lua-o-Ho'ohila. She could trace her lineage back to Mo'ikeha's brother, Kumu-honu-i'a-a-Muli'eleali'i, and to Ahukiniala'a. She owned the *kapu puhi kanaka* (the privilege to burn men who broke her *kapu*) as well as two inherited *kumu kanawai*, both of which gave her the right to drown any transgressors. She married Kākuhihewa of O'ahu, and when her cousin Kawelomahamahai'a created the *nī'aupi'o* rank, she sent her envoy to find out exactly what was happening. As a result, she was instrumental in arranging brother and sister marriages on Maui and O'ahu. Her grandson Kūali'i became the *ali'i nui* of Kaua'i after Kaweloleimakua was thrown to his death by his people. The *kapu* that Kūali'i inherited were so strict that this beach was declared sacred and a place of refuge. Any lawbreaker who could reach these sands could no longer be punished.[23]

Afterword

*O*nce Kūaliʻi became ruler of Kauaʻi, attention was paid to the wars raging on the windward islands. Kūaliʻi visited Kauaʻi once to survey it as a potential source of men and materiel. He was able to create a multi-island nation comprising Kauaʻi, Oʻahu, Molokaʻi, and part of Maui. Pele-io-hōlani followed his father as *aliʻi nui*. His daughter Kaʻapuwai, in turn, was installed as the *aliʻi nui*, and her daughter Ka-maka-helei followed her.

During the reign of Kamakahelei, James Cook discovered Kauaʻi in January 1778. He and subsequent European and American traders and explorers brought Western diseases and weapons, which proved equally fatal. It was an obscure chief of Hawaiʻi island who immediately grasped the concept of Western warfare in its weaponry and strategy. He gathered guns and men, built boats and armed them. In a few years, Kamehameha was ruler of all the islands except Kauaʻi and Niʻihau.

Kaumualiʻi followed his mother Kamakahelei to the throne. Twice Kamehameha tried to invade Kauaʻi and failed. However, Kaumualiʻi realized that he could not withstand Kamehameha's forces much longer and ceded his island.

In 1819, the ancient *kapu* system was destroyed at the instigation of Kaʻahumanu, Kamehameha's widow. The Hawaiians had seen that the foreigners disobeyed the *kapu* with no response from the gods. Foreign guns killed commoner and chief alike. The wars over the past century had killed many of the *aliʻi* and much of the old social order was gone. New diseases, such as measles and smallpox, killed indiscriminately. The arrival the following year of American missionaries brought a new god and new concepts in political and religious life.

In 1824, after the death of Kaumualiʻi, there was a desperate attempt to regain independence. As a result, the Kamehameha forces within two weeks killed or exiled almost all Kaua'i *ali'i* and their families. The ancient kingdom, Kaua'i Kuapapa, came to an end.

Since then, many changes have taken place, and much of the ancient life and history of the Polynesians who discovered this island and lived here for over fifteen hundred years has been entirely forgotten. Yet the place-names remain, and with them the names of chiefs and chiefesses, gods and demigods, men and women can be recalled and their stories retold and remembered—*nā pana kaulana o Kaua'i,* "the famous places of Kaua'i."

Notes

Introduction

1. For further information on the migrations of the Polynesians, see Abraham Fornander, *An Account of the Polynesian Race, Its Origins and Migrations, and the Ancient History of the Hawaiian People to the Times of Kamehameha*, Volume I (Rutland, VT: Tuttle, 1969 reprint); Patrick Vinton Kirch, *Feathered Gods and Fishhooks, An Introduction to Hawaiian Archeology and Prehistory* (Honolulu: University of Hawai'i Press, 1985); and Peter H. Buck, *Vikings of the Sunrise* (New York: Frederick A. Stokes, 1938).

2. Today the island's name is pronounced "Kau-a'i." According to Mary Kawena Pukui and Samuel H. Elbert in the *Hawaiian Dictionary* (Honolulu: University of Hawai'i Press, 1986 edition), the meaning could be *kau* (to place) and *a'i* (a transitivizer). Much earlier, William Ellis, in his *Polynesian Researches; Hawaii* (Rutland,VT: Tuttle, 1969 reprint) wrote: "The meaning of the word tauai [Kauai] is, to light upon, or to dry in the sun; and the name, according to the account of the late king, was derived from the long droughts which sometimes prevailed, or the large pieces of timber which have been occasionally washed upon its shores." He further pointed out that the correct pronunciation of Tau-ai is "Tow-i" or "Tow-eye."

East Kona District

1. William H. Rice, *Hawaiian Legends*, Bernice P. Bishop Museum Bulletin 3 (Honolulu: Bishop Museum Press, 1923), pp. 44–46.

2. Mary Kawena Pukui, *'Ōlelo No'eau, Hawaiian Proverbs and Poetical Sayings*, Bernice P. Bishop Museum Special Publication No. 7 (Honolulu: Bishop Museum Press, 1983) has **Ka-wai-'ula-'iliahi**, "red sandalwood water." Althea Kaohe (personal communication) told me this is incorrect; the saying stems from the fact that when one sticks any part of one's body into the water, one's skin appears to have turned a dark red. The same phenomenon can still be seen by plunging one's hand into the waters of Kawaikōī in the mountains.

3. Joseph A. Akina, "The Story of the Menehune People" (holographic manuscript transcribed by Frances Frazier, 1904). Rev. Akina's manuscript runs to 205 typewritten pages. It was written at the request of William H. Rice and certain portions of it were incorporated into Rice's *Hawaiian Legends*. The manuscript is privately owned by a descendant of W. H. Rice.

4. Fornander, *An Account of the Polynesian Race*, Vol. 1, pp. 77–78. Also Abraham Fornander, *Collection of Hawaiian Antiquities and Folk-lore*, Bernice P. Bishop Museum Memoirs 4, 5, and 6, edited by Thomas G. Thrum (Honolulu: Bishop Museum Press, 1916–1919), Vol. VI, p. 278.

5. Papaʻenaʻena is the name of the law forbidding the eating of human flesh, declared by Hawaiʻiloa after he discovered on his return to his homeland that his brother had accepted cannibalism. Fornander, *Collection of Hawaiian Antiquities and Folk-lore*, Vol. VI, p. 280.

6. There are many sources for the story of the Menehune Ditch (as it is called today). Thomas G. Thrum, "Who or What Were the Menehunes?" *(Hawaiian Almanac and Annual, 1929)* and C. B. Hofgaard, "Who Were the Menehunes?" (*Paradise of the Pacific*, May 1928) are good sources. For a detailed description of the ditch itself, see Wendell Clark Bennett, *Archeology of Kauai*, Bernice P. Bishop Museum Bulletin No. 80 (Honolulu: Bishop Museum Press, 1931).

7. Roland Gay, *Hawaii: Tales of Yesteryear* (Privately printed, 1977).

8. Fornander, *Collection of Hawaiian Antiquities and Folk-lore*, Vol. V, pp. 396–405.

9. Hiram Bingham, *A Residence of Twenty-One Years in the Sandwich Islands* (Hartford: Hezekiah Huntington, 1849).

10. Ralph S. Kuykendall, *The Hawaiian Kingdom, 1778–1854: Foundation and Transformation* (Honolulu: University of Hawaiʻi, 1938), page 434. Captain Joseph Ingraham, *Log of the Brig Hope* (May 26, 1791, Hawaiian Historical Society Reprints No. 3, pp. 15, 19) says that Captain William Douglas had left two men on Kauaʻi in August 1790.

11. George Vancouver, *A Voyage of Discovery to the North Pacific Ocean, and Round the World . . . in the years 1790, 1791, 1792, 1793, 1794, and 1795* (6 vols., London, 1801). Vancouver found these three men on Kauaʻi in March 1792.

12. Ibid.

13. In the records of the Māhele of 1848 to 1851, her name is spelled *Mere*, although today it would be corrected to *Mele*. Before the language was codified by the missionaries so that they could issue a translation of the Bible, they had to choose between the sounds used on the different islands. Kauaʻi used the *t* (as in tapa and tī). Early Western visitors wrote this island's name beginning with a *t*—Tauai. The letter *r* was used especially on the island of Hawaiʻi in place of the *l*. See William Ellis, *Polynesian Researches, Hawaii* (Rutland,

VT: Tuttle, 1984), Appendix, page 459; and Buck, *Vikings of the Sunrise*, pp. 242–243.

14. David Malo, *Hawaiian Antiquities*, Bernice P. Bishop Museum Special Publication 2, translated from the Hawaiian by Dr. Nathaniel B. Emerson (Honolulu: Bishop Museum Press, 1898), p. 116.

15. Fornander, *Collection of Hawaiian Antiquities and Folk-lore*. Vol. V, p. 274.

16. Henry P. Judd, *Hawaiian Proverbs and Riddles*, Bernice Pauahi Bishop Museum Bulletin 77 (Honolulu: Bishop Museum Press, 1930), No. 613.

17. Rice, *Hawaiian Legends*, p. 92.

18. Thelma H. Hadley and Margaret S. Williams, *Kauai, the Garden Island of Hawaii; and Guide Book* (Lihue, HI: Garden Island, 1962).

19. Pukui, *'Ōlelo No'eau*, No. 686.

20. Judd, *Hawaiian Proverbs and Riddles*, No. 627.

21. Ibid., No. 623.

22. Theodore Kelsey, *Kauai Place Names* (Kelsey Collection, State of Hawai'i Archives).

23. Ruth Hanner, *Early Waimea* (Kauai Historical Society Paper No. 89, 1952).

24. Ahuloulu can also be translated as "an altar made of *loulu*" or "an altar for placing *loulu* upon." The *loulu* is a member of the Pritchardia family of fan palms native to Hawai'i. According to Mary Kawena Pukui and Samuel H. Elbert, *Hawaiian Dictionary* (Honolulu: University of Hawai'i Press, 1986), *loulu* is also the name of a type of *heiau* specially built for services seeking the prevention of epidemics, famine, and destruction in general. If there is such a double meaning hidden in this name, it has been completely lost. This holds true for any *heiau* name.

25. Charles A. Rice, *Storyteller*. My grandfather had little difficulty holding an audience of youngsters enthralled as we made long journeys either by car or on horseback.

26. Ibid. This was the preferred version of my grandmother Grace King Rice, since it is less apt to be frightening to children.

27. Fornander, *Collection of Hawaiian Antiquities and Folk-lore*, Vol. V, pp. 580–583.

28. Mary Kawena Pukui, *Ancient Hulas of Kauai* (Kauai Historical Society Paper No. 62, 1936).

29. Judd, *Hawaiian Proverbs and Riddles*, No. 617 gives *Ua ia kaua e ka ua, hi kikii kaua i ka — nana*, "We are rained upon, we sit looking at it." This

proverb is quoted to mean "get out of the rain." Emerson, *Unwritten Literature*, p. 211 gives *Ki-ki'i ka ua i ka nana keia, la,* " 'Neath this bank I crouch sheltered from rain."

30. Francis Gay, *Place Names of Kauai* (Holographic unpublished manuscript, Hms. Misc. 4, Bernice P. Bishop Museum Archives, transcribed by M.W.).

31. Eric A. Knudsen, *Queen Emma Goes to Alakai Swamp* (Kauai Historical Society Paper No. 67, 1940).

32. *Papers by Lahainaluna Students,* No. 15 (Unpublished manuscript, Hms. Misc. 4, No. 1, Bernice P. Bishop Museum Archives, 1885).

33. Ibid.

34. Rice, *Hawaiian Legends,* p. 90.

35. Gay, *Place Names of Kauai.*

36. *A Collection of Voyages and Travels from the Discovery of America to the Commencement of the Nineteenth Century* (28 vols. London: Printed for Richard Phillips, Bridge Street, Blackfriars; by J. Gold, Shoe-land, 1809), Vol. XII, p. 154.

37. *Papers by Lahainaluna Students,* No. 15.

38. For an overview of the Russians on Kaua'i, see Edward Joesting, *Kauai, A Separate Kingdom* (Honolulu: University of Hawai'i Press, 1984); Peter R. Mills, "A New View of Kaua'i as 'The Separate Kingdom' after 1810" (*Hawaiian Journal of History* 30, 1966); and Kuykendall, *The Hawaiian Kingdom.*

39. Kuykendall, *Hawaiian Kingdom,* p. 14.

40. There are five major sources of the Kawelo legend: (1) Fornander, *Collection of Hawaiian Antiquities and Folk-lore,* Vol. V, pp. 2–71; (2) Fornander, *Hawaiian Antiquities and Folk-lore,* Vol. V, pp. 694–716; (3) Laura C. Green, *The Legend of Kawelo,* edited by Martha Warren Beckwith (Poughkeepsie, NY: Vassar College, 1929); (4) M. Jules Remy, *Contributions of a Venerable Native to the Ancient History of the Hawaiian Islands* (Reno: Outbooks, 1979); (5) Rice, *Hawaiian Legends.* All further references to this legend will be cited as "the Kawelo Legends."

41. *Papers by Lahainaluna Students,* No. 16.

42. Lyle A. Dickey, *The Stories of Wailua, Kauai* (Kauai Historical Society Paper 110, 1915).

43. Charles Nordhoff, *Northern California, Oregon, and the Sandwich Islands* (New York: Harper & Brothers, 1877).

44. Lorrin Andrews, *A Dictionary of the Hawaiian Language* (Rutland, VT:

Tuttle, 1974 reprint of 1865 edition). This story is found in the entry for the word *manele,* p. 384.

45. The Kawelo Legends.

46. Bingham, *A Residence of Twenty-One Years in the Sandwich Islands.*

47. This is the preferred translation of Gabriel I and Ilei Beniamina (personal communication).

48. James J. Jarves, *History of the Hawaiian or Sandwich Islands* (Boston: Tappan Dennet, 1843).

49. The Kawelo Legends.

50. Fornander, *Collection of Hawaiian Antiquities and Folk-lore,* Vol. V, pp. 332–333, 370–371.

51. L. W. Hart, "Kauai's Sacred Stones" *(Paradise of the Pacific,* December 20, 1907, pp. 22–23).

52. Bennett, *Archeology of Kauai,* Site 66.

53. Malo, *Hawaiian Antiquities,* p. 207.

54. Bennett, *Archeology of Kauai,* Site 67.

55. Fornander, *Collection of Hawaiian Antiquities and Folk-lore,* Vol. V, pp. 332–333, 370–371.

56. Ethel M. Damon, *Koamalu: A Story of Pioneers on Kauai and of What They Built in That Island Garden* (Honolulu: Privately printed, 1931).

57. Ibid.

58. Rice, *Storyteller.*

59. Eric A. Knudsen, *Teller of Hawaiian Tales* (Honolulu: Coca-Cola Bottling Co., ca. 1945).

60. Fornander, *Collection of Hawaiian Antiquities and Folk-lore,* Vol. V, pp. 136–153, 372–375.

61. Hadley and Williams, *Kauai, the Garden Island of Hawaii.*

62. Damon, *Koamalu.*

63. *Papers by Lahainaluna Students,* No. 19.

64. Ibid.

65. The Kawelo Legends.

66. *Papers by Lahainaluna Students,* No. 19.

67. Ibid.

68. Ibid.

69. "A Hawaiian Legend of a Terrible War between Pele-of-the-eternal-fires and Waka-of-the-shadowy-waters," translated by Mary Kawena Pukui (Bernice P. Bishop Museum Library, HEN Vol II:942–1008).

70. Kōloa is the preferred pronunciation today as it reflects the area's history of sugar manufacturing, which began in 1835 and ended in 1996. Yet the correct name may be Koloa, for a now extinct three-foot-high flightless bird whose skeleton has been found in this area.

71. Bennett, *Archeology of Kauai*, Site 83.

72. Akina, "Story of the Menehune People."

73. *Papers by Lahainaluna Students*, No. 19.

74. Fornander, *Collection of Hawaiian Antiquities and Folk-lore*, V:136–153, 372–375.

75. Gabriel I (personal communication).

76. G. H. Dole, "The Koloa Swamp" (*Islander* 1:12, May 21, 1875).

77. The many possible translations of the name *Kamaulele* illustrate the difficulty of such an attempt when the story of its naming is unknown. Some possibilities and the translators: **Ka-maʻu-lele**, "windblown *maʻu* fern" (translated by Keao NeSmith and Esther Mookini); **Ka-maʻū-lele**, "windblown dampness" (translation agreed upon as a possibility by Esther Mookini); **Ka-mau-lele**, "continual flying" (Mookini); **Ka-maʻumaʻau-kele**, "area in a rain forest from *wao maʻu kele*" (*kele* is perhaps a variant of *lele*) (Mookini); **Ka-mau-lele**, "To clear up as of rain, to pass by" (Mookini); **Kama-ulele**, "swiftly moving child" (author).

78. In the Māhele records for the island of Kauaʻi, small salt ponds are referred to as *kuakua paʻakai*. Today the correct word is considered to be *hāhā-paʻakai*.

79. Fornander, *Collection of Hawaiian Antiquities and Folk-lore*.

80. *Papers by Lahainaluna Students*, No. 19.

81. Bennett, *Archeology of Kauai*, Sites 87 and 88.

82. His Hawaiian Majesty King David Kalakaua, *The Legends and Myths of Hawaii, The Fables and Folk-lore of a Strange People* (Rutland, VT: Tuttle, 1972 reprint of 1888 edition).

83. Gabriel I (personal communication).

Puna District

1. Fornander, *An Account of the Polynesian Race*, Vol. II, pp. 45–56.

2. Rice, *Storyteller*.

3. *Papers by Lahainaluna Students*, No. 19.

4. Land Court Award to Kuaa.

5. The Kawelo Legends.

6. Fornander, *Collection of Antiquities and Folk-lore,* Vol. V, pp. 192–197.

7. Neal, *In Gardens of Hawaii,* p. 718.

8. Rice, *Storyteller.*

9. Fornander, *Collection of Antiquities and Folk-lore,* Vol. V, pp. 342–363; Rice, *Hawaiian Legends,* pp. 51–53; and Westerveld, *Legends of Old Honolulu,* pp. 261–267.

10. Emerson, *Unwritten Literature,* pp. 189–190.

11. William D. Westervelt, *Hawaiian Legends of Ghosts and Ghost-Gods* (Rutland, VT: Tuttle reprint, 1991), pp. 21–25.

12. Lyle Dickey, *The Portrait of Queen Hina* (carbon of typewritten manuscript, dated April 29, 1929, in author's collection). That each chiefess wore a specific color may well be an anachronism, an example of new concepts creeping into old stories told by modern storytellers. The idea of colors and flowers representing the various islands is a custom that was started in the 1920s as part of the Kamehameha Day festivities.

13. Rice, *Storyteller.*

14. Fornander, *Collection of Antiquities and Folk-lore,* Vol. V, pp. 214–225.

15. Rice, *Storyteller,* and Thrum, *More Hawaiian Folk Tales.*

16. Bennett, *Archeology of Kauai,* Site 99.

17. Damon, *Koamalu.*

18. Emerson, *Pele and Hiiaka.*

19. Akina, "Story of the Menehune People."

20. Kelsey, *Notes.*

21. Judd, *Hawaiian Proverbs and Riddles,* No. 615.

22. Pukui, *Ōlelo Noʻeau,* No. 2320.

23. *Papers by Lahainaluna Students,* No. 19. The names within the legend suggest that the correct name of the *heiau* has not reached us. Is it Ka-lei-o-ka-manu? Or Ka-lae-o-ka-manu? Or Ka-lau-o-kamani? The name also suggests this is a sister *heiau* to Ka-lei-o-manu in Wailua.

24. S. Aukai, "The Legend of Kealohiwai" (typewritten manuscript in author's possession).

25. Rice, *Hawaiian Legends.*

26. Thrum, *More Hawaiian Folk Tales.*

27. Punanuikaiaʻāina himself seems to have borne this name and there is a confusion as to whether Wailuanuiahoʻāno is the name of a particular chief, or of the land only, or both.

28. Fornander, *An Account of the Polynesian Race,* Vol. II, pp. 45–46.

29. Ibid.

30. Kalakaua, *The Legends and Myths of Hawaii*, pp. 125–131. It is claimed that a large covered calabash in the Bernice Pauahi Bishop Museum is actually La'amaomao's calabash, carefully preserved from the twelfth century.

31. Bennett, *Archeology of Kauai*, Site 107.

32. Pukui, *Ōlelo No'eau*, No. 467.

33. Dickey, *Stories of Wailua, Kauai.*

34. Fornander, *Collection of Antiquities and Folk-lore*, Vol. IV, pp. 160–177.

35. Buck, *Vikings of the Sunrise.*

36. Rice, *Hawaiian Legends.*

37. Dickey, *Stories of Wailua, Kauai*, and Andrews, Robert Standard, "A Legend of Kauai" (from the Hawaiian of A. H. Ahakuelo), *Paradise of the Pacific*, February to May, 1911.

38. Since the pronunciation of **Malae** and the story behind its naming are not known, it remains untranslatable into English. Mary Kawena Pukui, Samuel H. Elbert, and Esther T. Mookini, in *Place Names of Hawaii*, do not give a translation, although they translate **Māla'e**, the name of a *heiau* on Moloka'i, as "clear." The Mary Kawena Pukui and Samuel H. Elbert *Hawaiian Dictionary* has the following entries: "**Malae**. nvs. Malaya; Malay. *Eng.*" (the Hawaiianization of an English word, which clearly has no reference to this *heiau*); and "**māla'e**. Clear, calm; clear of weeds, as a field; serene, as a cloudless sky." An entry in *Papers by Lahainaluna Students, Record of a Tour of Kauai*, Hms. Misc. 43, No. 19, Wailua, September 14, 1885, gives this *heiau*'s name as **Malaea**, defined by Pukui-Elbert as "māla'ea, pas/imp of māla'e." The *heiau* is now in the path of a proposed new highway and therefore in danger of being destroyed in the name of progress.

39. Bennett, *Archeology of Kauai*, Site 104.

40. The true Kaua'i meaning of the name **Poli'ahu** is also not known. Poli'ahu means "a soft gentle touch, the gentle adherence of one thing to another" according to the Pukui-Elbert dictionary. Poli'ahu is also the name of the snow goddess who lived on Mauna Kea on Hawai'i. In Haleole's version of the legend of Lā'ie-i-ka-wai, she becomes the wife of 'Ai-wohi-kupua, a chief of Kaua'i. When he married another woman on the banks of the Wailua, she stood outside their honeymoon house and chilled them to the bone. Within a few days the new wife left for home.

41. Bennett, *Archeology of Kauai*, Site 106.

42. *Papers by Lahainaluna Students*, No. 15.

43. Dickey, *Stories of Wailua, Kauai.*

44. Ibid.

45. Ibid.

46. "A Hawaiian Legend of a Terrible War between Pele-of-the-eternal-fires and Waka-of-the-shadowy-waters."

47. Emerson, *Unwritten Literature,* and Dickey, *Stories of Wailua, Kauai.*

48. Dickey, *Stories of Wailua, Kauai.*

49. Ibid.

50. *Papers by Lahainaluna Students,* No. 19.

51. Dickey, *Stories of Wailua, Kauai.*

52. Ibid.

53. Theodore Kelsey, *Place Names from Mr. Isaac Ka'iu* (Kelsey Collection, Archives of Hawaii); Dickey, *Stories of Wailua, Kauai.*

54. Dickey, *Stories of Wailua, Kauai.*

55. Ibid.

56. Ibid.

57. The Kawelo Legends.

58. Rice, *Storyteller.*

59. Ibid.

60. The Kawelo Legends.

61. Dickey, *Stories of Wailua, Kauai.*

62. *Papers by Lahainaluna Students,* No. 19.

63. Kelsey, *Kauai Place Names.*

64. Emerson, *Unwritten Literature,* p. 40.

65. Ibid.

66. Dickey, *Stories of Wailua, Kauai.*

67. W. D. Westervelt, *Hawaiian Legends of Old Honolulu, Hawaii* (Rutland, VT: Tuttle, reprint 1963).

68. The Kawelo Legends.

69. Fornander, *Collection of Antiquities and Folk-lore,* Vol. IV, pp. 574–595.

70. Dickey, *Stories of Wailua, Kauai.*

71. Emerson, *Pele and Hiiaka.*

72. *Lahainaluna Students' Compositions,* No. 15.

73. Fornander, *Collection of Hawaiian Antiquities and Folk-lore,* Vol. 5, pp. 72–77.

74. Rice, *Storyteller.*

75. The Kawelo Legends.

76. Malo, *Hawaiian Antiquities*; Kalakaua, *The Legends and Myths of Hawaii*.

77. Akina, *History of the Menehune*.

78. The Kawelo Legends.

Ko'olau District

1. Andrews, *A Dictionary of the Hawaiian Language*, entry for *hao*, p. 134.

2. Daniel Akaka Jr., "Nā Kaikamāhine ā Pehuiki."

3. *The Hawaiian Romance of Laieikawai*.

4. Juliette L. Ferreira, "Lahemanu" (Story for the Martha W. Beckwith Prize, Kamehameha School for Girls, original paper, 1939).

5. Andrews, *A Dictionary of the Hawaiian Language*, Entry for "Kalalea," p. 251. Andrews says *ka-la-le-a* is the name of a fish of the eel kind on the mountain Kalalea; *oia ka ia ino ma ke Kalalea*.

6. Dickey, *String Figures*.

7. The Kawelo Legends.

8. Eliza Maguire, *Kauai* (typewritten journal of a trip to Kaua'i in 1925; private possession).

9. Rice, *Hawaiian Legends*.

10. Akina, "Story of the Menehune People."

11. Bennett, *Archeology of Kauai*, Site 124

12. Samuel Manaiakalani Kamakau, *Ka Po'e Kahiko, the People of Old*, translated from the Newspaper *Ke Au 'Oko'a* by Mary Kawena Pukui, arranged and edited by Dorothy B. Barrère (Bernice P. Bishop Museum Special Publication 51, Honolulu: Bishop Museum Press, 1964).

13. E. S. Craighill Handy and Elizabeth Green Handy, *Native Planters in Old Hawaii: Their Life, Lore, and Environment* (Bernice P. Bishop Museum Bulletin 233, Honolulu: Bishop Museum Press, 1978 reprint), p. 422.

14. Akina, "Story of the Menehune People."

15. Kelsey, *Place Names of Kauai*.

16. Rice, *Storyteller*.

17. Fornander, *Hawaiian Antiquities and Folk-lore*, Vol. V, p. 500.

18. Kelsey, *Place Names of Kauai*.

19. Juliette Ferreira, "Pele, the Goddess of Fire" (Story for the Martha W. Beckwith Prize, Kamehameha School for Girls, original paper, 1939).

20. Rice, *Hawaiian Legends*.

Halele'a District

1. Samuel M. Kamakau, *Ruling Chiefs of Hawaii* (Honolulu: The Kamehameha Schools Press, 1961), pp. 194–195; Bennett, *Archaeology of Kauai*, Site 147; and Land Court Award 9285, issued to Kekaululu, Kihei's wife.

2. Dickey, *Hanalei Place Names*.

3. *Winds of Kauai*, translated by M. K. Pukui (*Ka Na'i Aupuni*, June 18–20, 1906).

4. "Mu o Laau-haele-mai, the People Who Were Called the Banana Eaters," translated by Mary Pukui (*Aloha Aina-Puka La*, October 24, 1893 to December 19, 1893).

5. Rice, *Hawaiian Legends*, p. 47. See also Pukui, *'Ōlelo No'eau*, No. 404.

6. Kelsey, *Kauai Place Names*; Hashimoto, (personal communication); Juliet Rice Wichman, (personal communication).

7. Rice, *Hawaiian Legends*, pp. 7–17.

8. The Kawelo Legends.

9. *Māmala-hoe*, "splintered paddle," is the name of the law made about 1793 by Kamehameha I to guarantee the safety of travelers. Since then this name has been erroneously attached to this massif. The name Māmalahoa is far older by centuries than Kamehameha's experience on the road. Kamakau, *Ruling Chiefs of Hawaii*, p. 50, quotes the chant of Kapa'ihiahilina to Lonoikamakahiki wherein the name Mamalahoa is given. The attempt to equate this name with the conqueror, it seems to me, is an attempt to foist a victorious conquest upon a beaten people.

10. Akina, "Story of the Menehune People."

11. Dickey, *Hanalei Place Names*. The spelling used in the Hawaiian Bible is *Betelehema*, but Rev. Johnson, when writing the witness accounts for the Māhele in 1851, spelled it *Betelema*, and this spelling has continued to be used on Kaua'i. It has also been spelled *Kalema*.

12. Rice, *Hawaiian Legends*, pp. 47–48.

13. Fornander, *Collection of Hawaiian Antiquities and Folk-lore*, Vol. IV, pp. 64–66.

14. Rice, *Hawaiian Legends*, pp. 47–48.

15. Knudsen, *Teller of Hawaiian Tales*.

16. Dickey, *String Figures from Hawaii* (Bernice P. Bishop Museum, Bulletin 54, 1928), pp. 95–96.

17. Rice, *Hawaiian Legends,* p. 14.

18. *Winds of Kauai.*

19. Maka (personal communication).

20. Fornander, *An Account of the Polynesian Race,* Vol. I, pp. 196, 249; Vol. II, p. 275. The Kaua'i *'amakihi* is a small endemic honeycreeper having green-yellow feathers. The color of the feathers in a cape immediately marked its wearer as a Kaua'i *ali'i.*

21. Akina, "Story of the Menehune People."

22. Maka (personal communication).

23. Akina, "Story of the Menehune People."

24. Ibid.

25. Fornander, *Collection of Hawaiian Antiquities and Folk-lore,* Vol. IV, pp. 32–108.

26. Akina, "Story of the Menehune People."

27. Ibid.

28. *Mu o Laau-haele-mai.*

29. J. M. Lydgate, "The Affairs of the Wainiha Hui" *(Hawaiian Almanac and Annual, 1913).*

30. Maka (personal communication). He translated the name **Kalauhe'e** as "slimy clothes."

31. Fornander, *An Account of the Polynesian Race,* Vol. I, pp. 195, 249; Vol. II, p. 93.

32. Kelsey, *Place Names of Kauai.* See also Dickey, *String Figures from Hawaii,* p. 82.

33. Ibid.

34. Nathaniel B. Emerson, *Pele and Hiiaka, a Myth from Hawaii* (Honolulu, 1915); Rice, *Hawaiian Legends,* pp. 10–17; Fornander, *Collection of Hawaiian Antiquities and Folk-lore,* Vol. VI, pp. 343–344.

35. [Haleole] *Story of Lā'ieikawai.*

36. Land Court Award 7049 to Kekela.

37. Akina, "Story of the Menehune People."

38. Ibid.

39. Maka (personal communication).

40. Rice, *Hawaiian Legends,* p. 42.

41. Ibid, p. 32.

42. Maka (personal communication).

43. J. M. Lydgate, "Charm and Romance of Haena, Kauai: Some Dramatic Affairs of the Gods of Olden Days, Whose Errors Were Familiarly Human in Spite of Their Magical Powers" (*Paradise of the Pacific*, December 1922).

44. Akina, "Story of the Menehune People."

45. Lydgate, "Charm and Romance of Haena, Kauai."

46. Emerson, *Pele and Hiiaka*.

47. Lydgate, "Charm and Romance of Haena, Kauai."

48. Mary Kawena Pukui, *Ancient Hulas of Kauai* (Kauai Historical Society Paper No. 62, 1936).

Nāpali District

1. Judd, *Hawaiian Proverbs and Riddles*, No. 636.

2. Kalakaua, *The Legends and Myths of Hawaii*, pp. 175–205, and Malo, *Hawaiian Antiquities*, pp. 251–254.

3. Rice, *Hawaiian Legends*, pp. 42–44.

4. Kelsey, *Place Names of George Kalama of Papaaloa* (State of Hawaii Archives, Kelsey Collection, n.d.).

5. Ibid. See also Pukui, *ʻŌlelo Noʻeau*, Nos. 1517 and 2529.

6. Hashimoto (personal communication).

7. Pukui, *ʻŌlelo Noʻeau*, No. 1399.

8. Rice, *Hawaiian Legends*, pp. 42–43.

9. Gay, *Place Names of Kauai*, gives this translation. Kaeo NeSmith offers the translation "joyous light of the leaves."

10. "Kaehuikimano o Puuloa" (*Ke Au Hou*, January 18, 1911).

11. *The Hawaiian Romance of Laieikawai*.

12. Nancy Piilani, *Stories from Kalalau* (typewritten manuscript, Kauai Museum, Catherine Stauder Collection).

13. Rice, *Storyteller*.

14. Andrews, *A Dictionary of the Hawaiian Language*.

15. Fornander, *Collection of Antiquities and Folk-lore*, Vol. IV, pp. 160–177.

16. All names of Kalalau's trails are found in Gay, *Place Names of Kauai*. When his handwritten manuscript was typed by "MW" (Mary Wiggins?) at the Bishop Museum, almost all names were translated into English. Therefore I prefer to follow these translations, since M.W. could conceivably have conferred with Mr. Gay on any doubtful meanings. Certain words, such as *opuka* in the place-name **Kaopukaula**, "small red hole," do not appear in the Pukui-

Elbert dictionary. With such a formidable undertaking as a dictionary, it is understandable that many words were left out, but it is hoped that scholars are making a list of these as yet uncodified words for inclusion in future editions.

17. C. S. Dole, "National Park for Garden Island"; Gay, *Place Names of Kauai*. Pukui, Elbert, and Mookini, *Place Names of Hawaii*, give the name as Nā-keiki-a-nā-'i'iwi, "children of the 'i'iwi birds."

18. Rice, *Storyteller*.

19. Christopher B. Hofgaard, *The Story of Piilani* (Kauai Historical Society Paper No. 29, 1916).

20. Piilani, *Stories of Kalalau*.

21. Fornander, *Collection of Antiquities and Folk-lore*, Vol. VI: 344.

22. Pukui, *'Ōlelo No'eau*, No. 2833.

23. *The Hawaiian Romance of Laieikawai*.

24. G. D. Gilman, *Journal of a Canoe Voyage along the Kauai Palis, Made in 1845* (Papers of the Hawaiian Historical Society No. 14, Honolulu: *Paradise of the Pacific*, 1908).

25. Ibid.

26. Knudsen, *Teller of Hawaiian Tales*.

27. Rice, *Storyteller*.

28. *Winds of Kauai*.

29. Ruth Knudsen Hanner (personal communication). This is apparently another of those place-names that has been misinterpreted. *Awaawa*, according to Ruth Hanner, is a variant pronunciation of the word *awāwa* (valley). Both spellings and meanings are listed in the Pukui-Elbert dictionary. Mrs. Hanner said the name had nothing to do with ginger, *'awapuhi* (thus the rendering Awa'awapuhi as "ginger valley" given by Pukui, Elbert, and Mookini in *Place Names of Hawaii* is in error).

30. Knudsen, *Teller of Hawaiian Tales*.

31. Gay, *Place Names of Kauai*.

West Kona District

1. Isobel Faye, *Oral History* (Kauai Museum Collection).

2. *Winds of Kauai*.

3. Bennett, *The Archeology of Kauai*, Site 202.

4. Westervelt, *Hawaiian Legends of Old Honolulu*, pp. 204–245.

5. Fornander, *Collection of Hawaiian Antiquities and Folk-lore*, Vol. V, pp.

192–198. Today this name would be written as ʻUeʻuele-kēhau. There are many Kauaʻi words that contain "w" in their spelling.

6. Pukui, ʻŌlelo Noʻeau, No. 2910.

7. Hadley and Williams, Kauai, the Garden Island of Hawaii.

8. The sands of Nōhili are only one of two places in the world where the sands are said to bark. In reality, the sand motes are hollow, which is what causes the sound.

9. Rice, Storyteller.

10. Pukui, ʻŌlelo Noʻeau, No. 2135.

11. Bennett, Archeology of Kauai, Site 1.

12. Westervelt, Hawaiian Legends of Old Honolulu, pp. 82–89.

13. Pukui, ʻŌlelo Noʻeau, No. 2568.

14. "A Hawaiian Legend of a Terrible War between Pele-of-the-eternal-fires and Waka-of-the-shadowy-waters."

15. Fornander, Collection of Hawaiian Antiquities and Folk-lore, Vol. VI, pp. 266–281.

16. Pukui, ʻŌlelo Noʻeau, No. 112.

17. Knudsen, Teller of Tales.

18. The Hawaiian Romance of Laieikawai.

19. "A Hawaiian Legend of a Terrible War between Pele-of-the-eternal-fires and Waka-of-the-shadowy-waters."

20. Bennett, Archaeology of Kauai, Site 16; C. B. Hofgaard, Paper on Waimea (Kauai Historical Society Paper No. 4, September 17, 1914); Knudsen, Teller of Hawaiian Tales; Rice, No. 15; Thrum, More Hawaiian Folk Tales.

21. The five major sources of this legend are Beckwith, Hawaiian Mythology; Knudsen, Teller of Hawaiian Tales; Fornander, Hawaiian Antiquities and Folk-lore, Vol. V, p. 182; Thrum, Hawaiian Folktales; and Westervelt, Legends of Gods and Ghosts.

22. Beckwith, Hawaiian Mythology, pp. 272–275.

23. For information on Kahamaluʻihi (Ka-lua-i-Hoohila), see Fornander, An Account of the Polynesian Race, Vol. II, pp. 274, 275, 277.

Bibliography

Abbott, Isabella Aiona. *La'au Hawai'i: Traditional Hawaiian Uses of Plants.* Honolulu: Bishop Museum Press, 1992.

Akaka, Daniel, Jr. "Nā Kaikamāhine ā Pehuiki" (as told by Grandma Daisy Lovell) from Anahola, Kaua'i. Printed excerpt without source. (In private collection.)

Akina, Joseph A. "Seeing Lulu-o-Moikeha on the Plain of Kapa'a Once More." *Nupepa Kuokoa,* May 2, 1913. Translation by Mary K. Pukui. Bernice P. Bishop Museum Library.

———. "The Story of the Menehune People." Unpublished holographic manuscript in Hawaiian, transcribed by Frances Frazier, 1904. (In private collection.)

Andrews, Lorrin. *A Dictionary of the Hawaiian Language.* Rutland, VT: Tuttle, 1974 reprint.

Aukai, S. "The Legend of Kealohiwai." Typewritten manuscript. (In private collection.)

Barrère, Dorothy B., Mary Kawena Pukui, and Marion Kelly. *Hula: Historical Perspectives.* Pacific Anthropological Records No. 30, Department of Anthropology, Bernice P. Bishop Museum. Honolulu: Bishop Museum Press, 1980.

Beckwith, Martha Warren. *Hawaiian Mythology.* Honolulu: University of Hawai'i Press, 1970.

Bennett, Wendell Clark. *Archeology of Kauai.* Bernice P. Bishop Museum Bulletin No. 80. Millwood, NY: Kraus, 1976 reprint.

Berger, Andrew J. *Hawaiian Birdlife.* Honolulu: University Press of Hawai'i, 1972.

Bingham, Hiram. *A Residence of Twenty-One Years in the Sandwich Islands.* Hartford: Hezekiah Huntington, 1849.

Blanchard, Bill. "A Reef by Any Other Name." Interview with Henry Gomez. *Kauai Times,* January 7, 1987.

Buck, Peter H. *Vikings of the Sunrise.* New York: Frederick A. Stokes, 1938.

Carlquist, Sherwin. *Hawaii: A Natural History.* Lawai: Pacific Tropical Botanical Garden, 1980.

Certificates of Boundaries, Department of Accounting and General Services, State of Hawaii:

No. 2. Land of Kuiloa, District of Waimea, Island of Kauai.

No. 3. Land of Pilaa, District of Koolau, Island of Kauai.

No. 8. Kalaheo, Koloa, Kauai.

No. 9. Wahiawa, Koloa, Kauai.

No. 10. Lawai, Koloa, Kauai.

No. 11. Lumahai, Hanalei, Kauai.

No. 12. Waipaa, Hanalei, Island of: Kauai.

No. 13. Waioli, Hanalei, Island of: Kauai.

No. 14. Koula, Waimea, Kauai.

No. 15. Manuahi, Waimea, Kauai.

No. 16. Eleele, Waimea, Kauai.

No. 17. Land of Hanapepe, District of Waimea, Island of Kauai.

No. 18. Hanalei, Hanalei, Kauai.

No. 28. Waimea, Waimea, Kauai.

No. 29. Kikiaola, Waimea, Kauai.

No. 30. Kahili, Koolau, Kauai.

No. 31. Kalihiwai & Kalihikai, Halelea, Kauai.

Christensen, Charles. *Kaua'i's Native Land Shells*. Honolulu: Privately printed, 1992.

Clark, John R. K. *The Beaches of Kauai*. Honolulu: University of Hawai'i Press, 1989.

A Collection of Voyages and Travels from the Discovery of America to the Commencement of the Nineteenth Century. 28 vols. London: Printed for Richard Phillips, Bridge Street, Blackfrairs; by J. Gold, Shoe-land. 1809.

Damon, Ethel M. *Koamalu: A Story of Pioneers on Kauai and of What They Built in That Island Garden*. Honolulu: Privately printed, 1931.

Dickey, Lyle A. *Hanalei Place Names*. Kauai Historical Society Paper No. 105, 1934.

———. *The Portrait of Queen Hina*. Carbon of typewritten manuscript, April 29, 1929. (In private collection.)

———. *The Stories of Wailua, Kauai*. Kauai Historical Society Paper No. 110, 1915.

———. *String Figures from Hawaii Including Some from New Hebrides and Gilbert Islands*. Bernice P. Bishop Museum Bulletin 54. Millwood: Kraus, 1985 reprint.

Dole, C. S. "National Park for Garden Island." *Paradise of the Pacific*, December 1916: 50–55.

Earle, Timothy. *Economic and Social Organization of a Complex Chiefdom:*

The Halelea District, Kaua'i, Hawaii. Museum of Anthropology, University of Michigan, No. 63. Ann Arbor: University of Michigan Press, 1978.

Ellis, Harriet. "The Legend of Niumalu Fishpond." Hawaiian Legends Submitted by the Pupils of the Kamehameha School for Girls for the Martha Beckwith Prize, 1942.

Emerson, Nathaniel B. *Unwritten Literature of Hawaii: The Sacred Songs of the Hula, Collected and Translated with Notes and an Account of the Hula.* Rutland, VT: Tuttle, 1965 reprint.

Emory, Kenneth P. "The Ruins of Kee, Haena." Typewritten manuscript (in private collection).

Ferreira, Juliette L. "Lahemanu." Story for the Martha W. Beckwith Prize, Kamehameha School for Girls. Original paper, 1939.

———. "The Story of the Caterpillar." Hawaiian Legends Submitted by the Pupils of the Kamehameha School for Girls for the Martha Beckwith Prize, 1938.

Fielding, Ann, and Ed Robinson. *An Underwater Guide to Hawai'i.* Honolulu: University of Hawai'i Press, 1987.

Fornander, Abraham. *An Account of the Polynesian Race, Its Origins and Migrations, and the Ancient History of the Hawaiian People to the Times of Kamehameha I.* Rutland, VT: Tuttle, 1969 reprint.

———. *Collection of Hawaiian Antiquities and Folk-lore.* Edited by Thomas G. Thrum. B. P. Bishop Museum Memoirs 4, 5, 6. Honolulu: Bernice P. Bishop Museum, 1916–1919.

Gay, Francis. *Place Names of Kauai.* Typewritten transcription, Bernice P. Bishop Museum Library.

Gilman, G. D. *Journal of a Canoe Voyage along the Kauai Palis, Made in 1845.* Papers of the Hawaiian Historical Society No. 14. Honolulu: Paradise of the Pacific, 1908.

Green, Laura C. *The Legend of Kawelo.* Ed. Martha Warren Beckwith. Poughkeepsie, NY: Vassar College, 1929.

Hadley, Thelma H., and Margaret S. Williams. *Kauai, the Garden Island of Hawaii; and Guide Book.* Lihue, HI: Garden Island, 1962.

Handy, E. S. Craighill. *The Hawaiian Planter.* Vol. I. Bernice P. Bishop Museum Bulletin No. 161. Millwood: Kraus, 1985 reprint.

Handy, E. S. Craighill, and Elizabeth Green Handy. *Native Planters in Old Hawaii: Their Life, Lore, and Environment.* Bernice P. Bishop Museum Bulletin 233. Honolulu: Bishop Museum Press, 1972.

Hart, L. W. "Kauai's Sacred Stones." *Paradise of the Pacific* 20 (December 1907): 22–23.

"A Hawaiian Legend of a Terrible War between Pele-of-the-eternal-fires and Waka-of-the-shadowy-waters." Translated by Mary K. Pukui. *Ka Loea Kalaaina*, May 13–December 20, 1899. Bishop Museum Library.

The Hawaiian Romance of Laieikawai. With Introduction and Translation by Martha Warren Beckwith. Reprinted from the Thirty-Third Annual Report of the Bureau of American Ethnology, Washington, D.C.: Government Printing Office, 1918.

"He Wahi Moolelo Hawaii." Translated by Mary K. Pukui. *Nupepa Kuakoa*, June 27, 1902. Bishop Museum Library.

Hiroa, Te Rangi (Peter H. Buck). *Arts and Crafts of Hawaii.* Bernice P. Bishop Museum Special Publication 45. Honolulu: Bishop Museum Press, 1957.

Hofgaard, C. B. *Waimea.* Kauai Historical Society Paper No. 4, September 17, 1914.

———. "Who Were the Menehunes?" *Paradise of the Pacific,* May 1928.

Imlay, L. E. *Map of Kauai Compiled from Government Surveys and Private Surveys of Lands Belonging to Gay and Robinson.* State of Hawaii Surveyor's Office, Map. 2246, 1891.

[Ingraham, Captain Joseph.] *The Log of the Brig Hope Called The Hope's Track among the Sandwich Islands, May 20, October 12, 1791.* Hawaiian Historical Society Reprints, No. 3. Honolulu: *Paradise of the Pacific,* 1918.

Jarves, James J. *History of the Hawaiian or Sandwich Islands.* Boston: Tappan Dennet, 1843.

Joesting, Edward. *Kauai: A Separate Kingdom.* Honolulu: University of Hawai'i Press and Kauai Museum Association, 1984.

Johnson, Rubellite Kawena. *Kumulipo: Hawaiian Hymn of Creation.* Vol. I. Honolulu: Topgallant, 1981.

Judd, Henry P. *Hawaiian Riddles and Proverbs.* Bernice Pauahi Bishop Museum, Bulletin 77. Honolulu: Bishop Museum Press, 1930.

Kamakau, Samuel Manaiakalani. *Ka Po'e Kahiko, the People of Old.* Translated from the newspaper *Ke Au 'Oko'a* by Mary Kawena Pukui, arranged and edited by Dorothy B. Barrère. Bernice P. Bishop Museum Special Publication 51. Honolulu: Bishop Museum Press, 1964.

Kanoa, Charles K. "Nawailua." *Nupepe Kuokoa,* 1919.

"The Kapahi Stone." *Makahonu Naumu,* May 22, 1940. Bishop Museum Library.

Kauai Papers, The. Lihue: Kauai Historical Society, 1991.

Kawailiula, S. K. "A Short Story." *Ka Hae Hawaii,* October 9, 1861. Bishop Museum Library.

Kekahuna, Henry P. *Kauai Place Names.* Kekahuna Collection, Archives of Hawaii, n.d.

———. *Miscellaneous Papers.* Kekahuna Collection, Archives of Hawaii., n.d.

———. *Notes.* Kekahuna Collection, Archives of Hawaii, n.d.

———. *The Story of Ualakaa.* Kekahuna Collection, Archives of Hawaii, n.d.

Kelsey, Theodore. *Hanalei District.* Kelsey Collection, Archives of Hawaii, n.d.

———. *Kauai Place Names.* Kelsey Collection, Archives of Hawaii, n.d.

———. *Place Names from Mr. Isaac Ka'iu.* Kelsey Collection, Archives of Hawaii, n.d.

———. *Place Names of George Kalama of Papaaloa.* Kelsey Collection, Archives of Hawaii, n.d.

———. *Place Names of Luahiwa of Kaua'i.* Kelsey Collection, Archives of Hawaii, n.d.

Kirch, Patrick Vinton. *Feathered Gods and Fishhooks: An Introduction to Hawaiian Archeology and Prehistory.* Honolulu: University of Hawai'i Press, 1985.

Knudsen, Eric A. *Queen Emma Goes to Alakai Swamp.* Kauai Historical Society Paper No. 67, 1940.

———. *Teller of Hawaiian Tales.* Honolulu: Coca-Cola Bottling Co., ca. 1945.

Kuykendall, Ralph S. *The Hawaiian Kingdom, 1778–1854: Foundation and Transformation.* Honolulu: University of Hawai'i, 1938.

Land Commission:

Foreign Testimony. Vol. 12.

Foreign Testimony. Vol. 13.

Native Register. Index.

Native Register. Vol. 9. Translated by Frances Frazier.

Native Testimony. Vol. 11. Translated by Sarah Nakoa.

Native Testimony. Vol. 12. Translated by Sarah Nakoa.

Land Court Awards and Awardees. 552 L. Konia, Wainiha, 22 August 1854. Disputed by No. 11216, M. Kekauonohi (for L. Haalelea).

Land Deed. From Kaopukea and Kaikiapele to Kale Holmes. October 1858.

Luomala, Katharine. *The Menehune of Polynesia and Other Mythical Little People of Oceania.* Millwood, NY: Kraus, 1986 reprint.

Lydgate, John M. "The Affairs of the Wainiha Hui." *Hawaiian Almanac and Annual, 1913.*

———. "Charm and Romance of Haena, Kauai." *Paradise of the Pacific,* December 1922.

———. "Ka-umu-alii: The Last King of Kauai." Twenty-fourth Annual Report of the Hawaiian Historical Society for the year 1915. Honolulu: Paradise of the Pacific, 1916.

———. "The Winning of the Mu-ai-maia Maiden." *Hawaiian Almanac and Annual, 1913.*

Maguire, Eliza. *Kauai.* Typewritten copy of a journal of a trip to Kaua'i in 1925. (In private collection.)

Malo, David. *Hawaiian Antiquities.* Bernice P. Bishop Museum Special Publication 2. Second Edition. Translated from the Hawaiian by Dr. Nathaniel B. Emerson, 1898. Honolulu: Bishop Museum Press, 1951.

Maps, Department of Accounting and General Services, State of Hawaii:
Registered Map 168. *Webster's Study of Waimea, Kauai, Kuleanas.*
Registered Map 1364. *Plan of Survey Including the Crown Lands, Waiawaawa, Mokihana, Waimea, Kekaha, Pokii, Mana, Milolii, Nualolo, Waiawa Situated on the Island of Kauai.*
Registered Map 1365. *Pilaa Survey Division.*
Registered Map 1371. *Kauai.*
Registered Map 1378. *Plan of Anahola.* James W. Gay, Surveyor, May 1875.
Registered Map 1379. *Plan of Kuiloa, the Property of Mrs. Kapiolani Kalakaua.*
Registered Map 1395. *Map of the Island of Kauai, Hawaiian Islands.*
Registered Map 2686. *Ili of Waimea.*

Maps, Miscellaneous:
Princeville Ranch, Halele'a, Kauai, Hawaii, TMK: Zone 5, Sections 3, 4, and 5, Survey & Map by R. M. Towill Corporation, Under supervision of Marcellino P. Correa.
Princeville Ranch, Halele'a, Kauai, Hawaii, TMK: Zone 5, Sections 3, 4, and 5, Fourth Division, (Final Subdivision Map), Owner: Lihue Plantation Co., Map 1.

Maps, Tax. State of Hawaii: Island of Kauai.

Maps. U.S. Department of the Interior, Geological Survey. 1983: *Anahola Quadrangle.* Scale 1:24,000.

Haena Quadrangle. Scale 1:24,000.

Hanalei Quadrangle. Scale 1:24,000.

Hanapepe Quadrangle. Scale 1:24,000.

Kapaa Quadrangle. Scale 1:24,000.

Kekaha Quadrangle. Scale 1:24,000.

Koloa Quadrangle. Scale 1:24,000.

Lihue Quadrangle. Scale 1:24,000.

Makaha Point Quadrangle. Scale 1:24,000.

Waialeale Quadrangle. Scale 1:24,000.

Waimea Canyon Quadrangle. Scale 1:24,000.

Mea Kakau. "He wahi moolelo Hawaii." *Nupepa Kuokoa,* June 27, 1902.

Mills, Peter R. "A New View of Kaua'i as 'The Separate Kingdom' after 1810." *The Hawaiian Journal of History* 30 (1996): 91–104.

Munro, George C. *Birds of Hawaii.* Rutland, VT: Tuttle, 1960 reprint.

"Mu o Laau-haele-mai, the People Who Were Called the Banana Eaters." Translated by Mary Pukui. *Aloha Aina–Puka La,* October 24, 1893 to December 19, 1893, Bishop Museum Library.

"Na Iliili Hanau o Koloa." *Nupepe Kuokoa,* February 10, 1911. Bishop Museum Library.

"Na Makani o Kauai." *Ka Na'i Aupuni,* June 18–26, 1906. Translated by Mary Kawena Pukui. Collection of Francis Frazier.

Neal, Marie C. *In Gardens of Hawaii.* Bernice P. Bishop Museum Special Publication 50. Honolulu: Bishop Museum Press, 1965.

Nordhoff, Charles. *Northern California, Oregon, and the Sandwich Islands.* New York: Harper & Bros., 1877.

Papers by Lahainaluna Students after Interviews with Old Residents of Kauai, 1885. Bernice P. Bishop Museum Archives. Lahainaluna Students Papers. Hms. Misc. 43:

No. 15. *Heiaus, Kauai, Fishing Grounds, Deep Fishing Grounds for Letting Down Ropes, The Surfs of Waimea, Why This Surf Was Famous, Secret Caves of Waimea, The Heiaus of Waiawa, The Heiaus of Kekupua, Pools Belonging to Chiefs.*

No. 16. *Information on Ancient Heiaus and Famous Stones of Religious Significance.*

No. 18. *Fishing Grounds outside of the Surf of Makaiwa as Far as Wailua, Heiaus of and Kapaa, Well-known Things, Famous Things Mentioned by Two Men, Heiaus from Kapaa to Kealia.*

No. 19. *Heiaus and Fishing grounds, Heiaus of Koloa, Fishing Grounds of Koloa, Record of a Tour of Kauai (Heiaus and Fishing Grounds) 1885, The Heiaus of Nawiliwili, September 16, 1885.*

Portlock, Nathaniel. *A Voyage Round the World, Particularly to the North-west Coast of America: Performed in 1785, 1786, 1787 and 1788, in The King George and Queen Charlotte by Captains Portlock and Dixon.* London: Printed for John Stockdale, opposite Burlington House, Piccadilly; and George Goulding, James Street, Covent Garden, 1794.

Pukui, Mary Kawena, *Ancient Hulas of Kauai.* Kauai Historical Society Paper No. 62, 1936.

———. *'Ōlelo No'eau: Hawaiian Proverbs and Poetical Sayings.* Bernice P. Bishop Museum Special Publication No. 71. Honolulu: Bishop Museum Press, 1983.

Pukui, Mary Kawena, and Samuel H. Elbert. *Hawaiian Dictionary* (Third Edition). Honolulu: University of Hawai'i Press, 1986.

———. *Place Names of Hawaii.* Honolulu: University of Hawai'i Press, 1966.

Pukui, Mary Kawena, Samuel H. Elbert, and Esther T. Mookini. *Place Names of Hawaii* (Second Edition). Honolulu: University of Hawai'i Press, 1974.

Remy, M. Jules. *Contributions of a Venerable Native to the Ancient History of the Hawaiian Islands.* Reno: Outbooks, 1979 reprint.

Rice, William Hyde. *Hawaiian Legends.* Bernice P. Bishop Museum, Bulletin No. 3. Honolulu: Bishop Museum Press, 1923.

Rock, Joseph F. *The Indigenous Trees of the Hawaiian Islands.* Lawai: Pacific Tropical Botanical Garden and Rutland, VT: Tuttle, 1974 reprint.

Schmitt, Robert C. "The Population of Northern Kauai in 1847." In *Hawaii Historical Review: Selected Readings,* ed. Richard A. Green. Honolulu: Hawaiian Historical Society, 1969.

Scott, Susan. *Plants and Animals of Hawaii.* Honolulu: Bess Press, 1991.

Stillman, Charles K., compiler. *Hawaiian Place Names—Kauai.* Unpublished manuscript in the possession of Ruby Scott and Mary Luddington.

Stokes, John F. G. *New Bases for Hawaiian Chronology.* Forty-First Annual Report of the Hawaiian Historical Society for the Year 1932.

Thrum, Thomas G. *Hawaiian Folktales.* Chicago: McClurg, 1907.

———. *More Hawaiian Folktales: A Collection of Native Legends and Traditions.* Chicago: McClurg, 1923.

———. "Who or What Were the Menehunes?" *Hawaiian Almanac and Annual,* 1929: 83–88.

Titcomb, Margaret. *Native Use of Fish in Hawaii.* Honolulu: University of Hawai'i Press, 1972.

Vancouver, George. *A Voyage of Discovery to the North Pacific Ocean, and Round the World, in the Years 1790, 1791, 1792, 1793, 1794 and 1795.* Six vols. London. 1798.

Westervelt, W. D. *Hawaiian Historical Legends.* New York: Fleming H. Revell, 1923.

———. *Hawaiian Legends of Ghosts and Ghost-Gods, Collected and Translated from the Hawaiian.* Rutland, VT: Tuttle, 1963 reprint.

———. *Legends of Gods and Ghosts.* Boston: Geo. H. Ellis, 1915.

———. *Legends of Old Honolulu, Hawaii.* Boston: Geo. H. Ellis, 1915.

Wichman, Frederick B. *Kauai Tales.* Honolulu: Bamboo Ridge Press, 1985.

———. *More Kaua'i Tales.* Honolulu: Bamboo Ridge Press, 1997.

———. *Polihale and Other Kaua'i Legends.* Honolulu: Bamboo Ridge Press, 1991.

Wilkes, Charles. *Narrative of the United States Exploring Expedition during the years 1838, 1839, 1840, 1841, 1842.* Philadelphia: Lea and Blanchard, 1845.

Index

About the Author

Frederick B. Wichman grew up in Wailua
on the island of Kaua'i. Author of *Kaua'i
Tales* and *Polihale and Other Kaua'i Tales,*
he frequently gives lectures and readings
concerning the stories and place-names of
his home island. He lives at Hā'ena, a land
rich with legends.